ICONIC

WATCHES

Quarto

First published in 2025 by Ivy Press,
an imprint of The Quarto Group.
One Triptych Place, London, SE1 9SH,
United Kingdom
T (0)20 7700 9000
www.Quarto.com

EEA Representation, WTS Tax d.o.o., Žanova ulica 3,
4000 Kranj, Slovenia.

A catalogue record for this book is available from the
British Library.

ISBN 978-1-83600-280-2
Ebook ISBN 978-1-83600-281-9

10 9 8 7 6 5 4 3 2 1

Design by Mat Wiggins
Publisher: Richard Green
Senior Editor: Laura Bulbeck
Picture Research: Stephen Behan, Róisín Duffy,
Laura Bulbeck
Senior Designer: Renata Latipova
Senior Production Manager: Alex Merrett

Printed in China

ICONIC

WATCHES

& THEIR

INCREDIBLE STORIES

COLIN SALTER

IVY PRESS

Contents

A Very Brief History of Time

In the beginning there was only daylight and darkness, the two phases of time every day which were all that early man needed, to know what to do when. That's fine for everyday activities like eating and sleeping. For less frequent events, there was the Moon in all its phases. The Moon, the tides and the menstrual cycle gave us useful markers for the passing time, and for the really long-term stuff, there were the annual seasons.

It was when we began to need divisions of less than a single day that humanity had to start being inventive. The sundial had its limits – cloudy days in some parts of the world and night-times everywhere. One early solution was the burning of candles – a wax column of a set diameter will burn down at a roughly predictable rate of so many centimetres an hour.

An hour was for many centuries a small enough unit by which to mark the day's work periods or religious prayers. The first mechanical clocks – powered by water or springs – showed only hours; but the invention of the pendulum movement in the mid-seventeenth century made accuracy possible to within a minute or so a day.

Human ingenuity being what it is, the earliest seconds dials appeared on clocks in the 1670s, long before anyone except alchemists had any use for such a small measurement. By 1800, the finest clockmakers where producing stopwatches capable of measuring single hundredths of a second.

Portable clocks

There are larger clocks and smaller clocks, but one has to be within sight of one to tell the time from it. Pocket watches were the first portable timepieces and made it possible to measure the length of a journey, for example. Timed observations were crucial to the improved accuracy of navigation at sea, and a portable clock meant that a sailor could take readings above deck and convey them to the navigator below. Landlocked Swiss clockmaker Ulysse Nardin made his name with the production of such marine timepieces.

The oldest known wristwatch (see page 10) was little more than a piece of animated jewellery built into a brightly decorated bracelet. The watch, 'mounted on a wristlet of hair woven with gold thread, simple gold key, a second wristlet, also woven with gold', was made for the Queen of Naples in 1810 by the legendary Parisian watchmaker Abraham-Louis Breguet.

It is entirely appropriate that the watchmaking industry, whose business is time, should continue to revere those at the very start of its timeline. Breguet is one of many early craftsmen whose names survive in the brands of today. Others include Blancpain, Patek Philippe, Panerai, Jaeger-LeCoultre and Junghans, all with histories stretching back between 150 and 200 years.

Watches were, for a century after the Queen of Naples, chiefly the luxury accessory of women, whether on the wrist or in a brooch. Marie Antoinette used to wear three distributed about her clothing, although she never got to wear the watch that bears her name (see page 14) – this, also made by Breguet, was only completed after her unfortunate death, and the story of its journey, disappearance and rediscovery from then until today has all the elements of a great historical novel.

Men did not wear wristwatches. Men were the workers of the world, out there getting their hands dirty in the school of hard knocks. Whether shearing a sheep or swinging a sabre, men's wrists were too vulnerable to blows to risk putting a watch on them. Pocket watches were universal among men, tucked safely out of harm's way in the pocket of a waistcoat and produced with a flourish when a time check was needed. The American Watch Company (see page 18) made the pocket watch, it was said, on which America's trains ran. A century later the Omega Railmaster was designed to appeal to the same market as well as other engineers and physicists.

Soldiers, pilots and divers

World War One, the first test of 'modern' warfare, saw a loss of life on an unimaginable scale. Like all wars, however, it encouraged innovation and stimulated changes in human behaviour. Large-scale coordinated attacks on the enemy required synchronized timing from the many units involved; and at the same time, soldiers on the front line needed their hands free to leap into action at the given moment.

They may have taken their cue from the army of nurses required to patch them up and get them back to the front as soon as possible – nurses were already in the habit of wearing their watches on their wrists or lapels. Wristwatches for men took off during this conflict and pocket watches suffered a long slow decline in sales for the rest of the twentieth century.

One of the first groups of men to see the benefits of a wristwatch were the pilots. Flight was still in its infancy and the controls of aircraft were mechanical and many. Pilots dare not remove their hands from the controls to consult a watch, and yet, like the sailors before them, relied on time to navigate the aircraft accurately, and to inform them when they were running out of fuel. Louis Cartier's 1904 design for his friend, the pioneer pilot Alberto Santos-Dumont (see page 22), was the first pilots' watch, and – coming from Cartier – a design classic. The Longines Lindbergh Hour Angle watch (see page 34) was another early contribution to the challenge of aerial navigation.

Now that men were wearing watches, the design of specialist watches for specific activities began in earnest. One of the first fields for innovation was in watches for the use of divers. Water ingress in the tiny mechanical workings of a timepiece meant rust and the end of the watch; and several makers had addressed the problem of waterproofing in the nineteenth century. Rolex boldly claimed the prize for being completely waterproof with its famous Oyster watch in 1926 (see page 30). But it's one thing to keep the rain out and another to withstand water pressure at depths of 30m (98.4ft), 20m (65.6ft), or even 10m (32.8ft) below the surface of the sea.

The drive for a reliable diver's watch was again spurred by military action. Divers were involved in some of the most daring covert acts of espionage of World War One, and Omega, Rolex and Blancpain have been friendly rivals in the perfection of the divers' watch ever since. The Omega Marine trumped the Rolex Oyster in 1932 when it was tested 75m (246ft) down at the bottom of Lake Geneva. Some divers' watches were so effective, like the Panerai Radiomir (see page 46), that they were military secrets – Panerai, first conceived for the Italian navy's secret underwater assaults on British ships, finally went public in 1993. Russia's equivalent, the Vostok Amphibia, was forced to find new markets after the collapse of the Soviet Union in 1991.

Making a movement

One thing that watchmakers have not yet mastered is perpetual motion. There has to be a source of power to make the hands go round. Clockwork, driven by an uncoiling spring which had to be rewound every day or week, was effective, and it became a matter of habit to wind one's watch last thing at night. There are plenty of watch purists who will still tell you that a hand-wound mechanical watch is still the only proper watch.

For those of us who either forgot to wind our watches or overwound them and damaged the spring, the development of the automatic watch was a godsend. The idea of harnessing the motion of the very wrist on which the watch is being worn has been explored by many manufacturers over the ages, and even in Marie Antoinette's time there were attempts to solve the problem. The great Breguet managed to make what the French called a *perpétuelle*, using an oscillating weight, although it was so bulky that it had to be housed in a large pocket watch.

The honour for the design of the first reliable automatic watch goes to a quiet Englishman, John Hardwood, who fought in World War One and afterwards invented a perpetual watch movement, inspired – he said – by seeing two children playing on a see-saw. He took the idea to Switzerland, where it went into production, only to be ruined by the Great Depression which soon followed its launch. Rolex took Hardwood's concept and ran with it, launching the world's first successful automatic movement in a version of the Oyster in 1931.

One tiny crystal

Clockmakers have always had to deal with the demands of finance, economy and fashion, just like any other industry. Some like Hardwood went under; many others survived. However, one single development in the way watches were powered threatened to demolish the entire traditional watchmaking industry almost overnight.

The arrival from Japan of the quartz watch, in the form of the Seiko Quartz-Astron 35SQ (see page 94), was an earthquake; and yet the technology behind it was almost a hundred years old – Pierre Curie, husband of the more famous Marie, had discovered the piezo-electric qualities of quartz in 1880; and the big players of the Swiss watch industry had been trying to harness it in a wristwatch since 1962.

Seiko won the race, with a watch which cost the equivalent of a mid-price family car. But the price soon came down and traditional Swiss manufacturers simply could not compete. In what became known as the Quartz Crisis, between 1970 and 1983, the number of individual watchmaking firms dropped from 1,600 to 600, and the number of employees, 90,000 in 1970, fell to 28,000 by 1988.

To its great credit, and with a little strong-arming from Swiss banks afraid of losing everything, Switzerland managed to regroup and consolidate what remained of its watch industry. Many of the major surviving companies joined forces in what would eventually become the Swatch Group. Unable to fight Japan on price, they took the traditional watch decidedly upmarket. Watches, which began life as the luxury accessories of wealthy women, were now aimed squarely at wealthy men and associated with other luxury activities like fast cars and sports. Today, not all those who wear divers' and pilots' watches are divers and pilots; instead, the watches they wear promote image, manliness and success. Perhaps it's a sign of the greater equality of the sexes that Hublot launched a women's version of its macho Big Bang watch (see page 130) in 2008, which now accounts for 28 per cent of its sales.

The Swatch Group is most famous, of course, for the Swatch watch (see page 114), a shrewd development which combined a very simple core movement – a Swatch watch has only 51 components – with infinite interchangeability of colour and design. It is the group's riposte to Japanese quartz, and by a succession of new designs and limited editions, it has made its own contribution to the survival of the Swiss industry.

The future and the past

Mind you, it has a long way to go to rival the Casio F-91W (see page 118), which has sold more than 100 million pieces since its introduction in 1989 and in some countries still costs the same today as it did back then. Digital watches have presented another challenge to the traditional industry, and now smartwatches do too. It feels sometimes as if it's only a matter of time before all the functions of watches, phones, computers and health monitors will be combined in a chip implanted somewhere in our heads.

The craftsmanship and history behind the modern watch industry resonate within the timepieces themselves. They speak of ingenuity, innovation and style. The greatest designs speak, ironically, of timelessness, of a beauty unaffected by fashion. Anything rare is collectable; and, with a timeline stretching back more than a quarter of a millennium, watches are now an object of desire for those with the collector's gene. A watch need not be expensive or even rare to be collectable, and a watch's individual narrative can contribute as much as its rarity to its value. Crimes have been committed for the possession of watches that once belonged to John Lennon (see page 66) and Marie Antoinette, for example.

This book looks at some of the milestones in the history of watches – the innovative, the expensive, the beautiful, and in the case of the Mickey Mouse watch (see page 42), the simply popular. Whatever watch you wear, it is the product of 250 years of ingenious human endeavour; take the time to enjoy it, and this book.

Breguet No. 2639 (1810)

It is appropriate that the world's first wristwatch was one fit for a queen to wear – and not just a queen, but the sister of an emperor. Unfortunately, the watch is lost, but thanks to some impressive nineteenth-century book-keeping by the manufacturer, historians know a great deal about watch No. 2639.

Abraham-Louis Breguet, born in Switzerland in 1747, was the finest watchmaker of his day. His mother remarried after his father's early death, and perhaps Breguet resented the arrival of his stepfather, Joseph Tattet, a clocksmith with a showroom in Paris. Certainly, for some time the young Abraham-Louis resisted Tattet's well-meaning attempts to interest him in the business and give him a good start in a skilled craft.

When he was aged 15, however, he agreed to be apprenticed to a watchmaker in Versailles. The year was 1762, the French royal family was still in charge, and watchmakers naturally clustered round the royal palace at Versailles in the hope of receiving a commission. Breguet showed great aptitude during his apprenticeship and while still indentured was introduced to the king himself, Louis XVI, for whom he completed several commissions including an impressive self-winding pocket watch, a *perpétuelle*.

Permitted to marry only when his apprenticeship was complete, he chose the daughter of a wealthy bourgeois merchant. The dowry which accompanied her was enough for Breguet to set up his workshop on the Quai de l'Horloge – Clock Quay – in the heart of Paris, where he continued to do business for the rest of his life.

After the French Revolution of 1789, Breguet was lucky not to be prosecuted for his connection with the overthrown royal family. He was indeed listed for the guillotine, but a fortunate friendship with the revolutionary leader Jean-Paul Marat, who came from the same part of Switzerland, helped him to escape that grisly fate.

Breguet invented several ingenious improvements to the mechanisms of clocks and pocket watches. No doubt his reputation as a skilled craftsman stood him in good stead in post-revolutionary France; and where once kings and queens had commissioned him, now the Emperor of France beat a path to his workshop door. Napoleon Bonaparte ordered many timepieces from Breguet and he carried them with him on his military campaigns. A recommendation from the Emperor carried almost as much weight as one from a king.

It was to be expected, therefore, that Napoleon's sister Caroline would find her way to the Quai de l'Horloge one day in 1810. Caroline was married to Joachim Murat, a military commander who had served with success and honour under Napoleon and was rewarded with a string of prestigious titles –

Caroline Bonaparte (1782–1839), Queen of Naples and Sicily, with her daughter Letizia, in an 1807 portrait by Marie Louise Élisabeth Vigée-Lebrun (1755–1842).

Breguet's twenty-first-century evocation of the Queen of Naples' watch, called the Reine de Naples collection, launched in 2019.

Abraham-Louis Breguet (1747–1823) at his desk, working on a watch, from a nineteenth-century French print.

Marshal of the Empire, Admiral of France, Prince Murat, Duke of Cleves and Grand Duke of Berg. Finally in 1808 Napoleon made him King of Naples, which made Caroline a queen.

The story from now on is recorded in the order books of Abraham-Louis Breguet and his son Antoine-Louis, which are preserved to this day in Paris. They are meticulous in their detail and although the present whereabouts of Caroline's watch are unknown, a great deal can be learned about it from the descriptions of it and the repairs made to it on several occasions.

From Breguet's order book we know that Caroline placed two orders on 8 June 1810. One was for a carriage clock, costing 100 Louis. (It's interesting that the price is recorded in Louis, a coin struck by French kings and worth 20 French francs. After Breguet's old client Louis XVI was beheaded, the coins were officially renamed Napoleons.) The other was for 'a repeater watch for bracelet for which we shall charge 5,000 francs'. A repeater is a watch that chimes.

Another book, recording the stages of manufacture, confirms that the watch (now order no. 2639) is to be oval and on a bracelet. This was unusual: watches were often worn as brooches but never before on the wrist and were rarely oval. Work on the timepiece began two months later, on 11 August – Breguet was, after all, a busy man – and through progress reports we know that 17 members of his staff took part in the 34 stages of its construction. These included the assembly of its quarter-repeater and of a thermometer which was built into the case, a rare complication even today.

The watch was completed in December 1811 and Breguet drew up an invoice for 4,800 francs. Perhaps the Queen of Naples had already paid a deposit of the other 200. Unexpectedly, Breguet did not deliver the watch for another year – there was a problem with the movement, which had to be replaced; and Caroline decided she wanted a dial of silver instead of gold. The dial was intricately engraved and had Arabic numerals. Roman numerals were more common, being easier to engrave because they were composed of straight lines.

The watch was finally ready on 21 December 1812, just in time for Christmas in Naples. Caroline was on her own, ruling in her husband's absence while he was fighting in Napoleon's disastrous Russian campaign. It was Joachim Murat's failure to provide the correct hoofwear for his horses that caused such problems for the French armies retreating on icy roads.

Murat was eventually executed by Napoleon's enemies and Caroline fled to safety in Austria. Queen no more, she took the title Countess of Lipona (an anagram of Napoli, the Italian form of Naples). She died in Florence in 1839. But the watch reappeared 10 years later when it was brought back to the Breguet workshop for repair on 8 March 1849 by the Countess Risponi. The countess was Louise, Caroline's youngest daughter, who married the Count Risponi and inherited her mother's watch.

Breguet had died in 1823 and there was great interest in the return of watch No. 2639 to its place of birth. In the repair records it was described in great detail: 'Very thin repeater watch No. 2639, silver dial, Arabic numerals, thermometer and fast/slow indicator off the dial, the said watch is mounted on a wristlet of hair woven with gold thread, simple gold key, a second wristlet, also woven with gold, in a red leather case.' Three weeks later the watch was returned to its owner, at a charge of 80 francs, with a report on the work done: 'We polished the pivots, reset the thermometer, restored the repeater to working order, overhauled the dial, cleaned each of the parts and adjusted the watch.' It returned to the Quai de l'Horloge one more time, in 1855, for further repairs; and that is the last record of its existence.

Thirteen years passed after that last sighting before the second wristwatch in history was made, by Patek Philippe for the Countess Koscowicz of Hungary. Although there is no visual record of the appearance of Queen Caroline's watch, today Breguet produces a modern range of oval bracelet watches under the name Reine de Naples.

The Marie Antoinette: Breguet Grande Complication No. 160 (1827)

What do you do when the rarest watch in the world is stolen and disappears from sight? And what possible connection does it have with the head of the Swatch brand of mass-produced watches and the felling of an old French oak?

Most of the watches in this book are mass-produced to a greater or lesser extent, and available to anyone with enough money to buy one. This is the story of a unique one-off with a royal pedigree, one whose story is bound up with one of the most tempestuous times of European history. As befits a history with such grand connections, there are many versions of the story of this watch. Here is one of them.

Hans Axel von Fersen was a cavalry general, a Swedish count who held the highest office in the royal Swedish court. He served as aide-de-camp to General Rochambeau, the French general who played a decisive role in defeating the British at Yorktown during the American War of Independence. In France he is said to have embarked on an enduring love affair with the French queen Marie Antoinette in 1774. Some of their correspondence survives and reveals a very intense emotional if not physical intimacy.

Marie Antoinette liked watches. A portrait of her from 1785 shows her with two fob watches hanging from her waist. At the time, clockwork mechanisms had been applied to a variety of functions, including a perpetual calendar, a display of celestial time, a chronograph, a minute repeater, a second hand, chimes and even a form of automatic winding. Never had they all been encompassed in a single timepiece; but when in 1783 Marie Antoinette expressed a desire for such a multi-function instrument, Fersen immediately commissioned one from a favourite watchmaker of the queen, Abraham-Louis Breguet.

Breguet's Paris workshop stood, appropriately, on the Quai de l'Horloge (Clock Quay). The street, on the Île de la Cité, is named after the city's first public clock, installed on the Palais de Justice in 1370. Fersen told Breguet to spare no expense in realizing the queen's wish, and Breguet took him at his word.

Although Fersen had set neither a budget nor a delivery date, it was becoming clear that the days of the French monarchy were numbered. The French Revolution erupted in 1789, and the queen, the intended recipient of the ambitious watch, was sent to the guillotine in 1793. Fersen had last visited Marie Antoinette in prison 10 days before her death and, being associated so intimately with her, wisely returned to his native Sweden. Breguet too was in danger of being beheaded for his royal connections, and in 1793 he too fled, first to his birthplace in Switzerland and later to England, where his French credentials found him work for King George III.

The reconstruction of Abraham-Louis Breguet's No. 160 Grande Complication on display in Jerusalem's L.A. Mayer Museum.

Marie Antoinette (1755–93), Queen of France, walking with two of her children in the Parque de Trianon, in a portrait by Adolf Ulrik Wertmüller (1751–1811). In it, she appears to be wearing two fob watches.

The painstaking reconstruction, from photos and diagrams, of Breguet's No. 160 was given the reference No. 1160.

When the worst terrors of the Revolution had subsided, Breguet returned to the Quai de l'Horloge, and to watch No. 160 – the number assigned to Fersen's commission. Breguet worked on, despite the deaths of Marie Antoinette and Fersen, but in 1823, Breguet himself died. Out of respect for the great watchmaker, however, his staff laboured on, and Breguet No. 160, with a movement so ingenious, so intricate that it became known as *la grande complication*, was at last signed off in 1827. Fersen had stipulated that any part that could be made of gold *should* be made of gold – Breguet himself chose rose gold to reflect the queen's femininity. With so many functions, the watch was double-sided – two glasses of clear rock crystal engraved with the numbers and dials necessary to read it. There were no opaque faces concealing the watch's workings – why hide such a masterpiece of horology? It has been estimated that the finished item cost the Breguet workshop between 17,000 and 30,000 francs to make. One pupil of Breguet, who worked on the watch mechanism for three years during his master's lifetime, was paid 7,250 francs for his contribution alone.

The workshop did indeed find a buyer. The sale is not recorded in Breguet's accounts, but in 1838 a surviving member of the French aristocracy, the Marquis de la Groye – who as a child had been one of Marie Antoinette's page boys – brought the watch in for a service. Now an old man, the marquis died before he could collect the watch and it returned into the ownership of the Breguet family, who kept it and the family business going until 1887. When Abraham-Louis Breguet's great-grandsons showed no interest in running the business it was sold to an English watchmaker, Edward Brown, whose descendants ran it until 1970. The Marie Antoinette, as watch No. 160 had become known, was sold to an English collector, Sir Spencer Brunton, for £600 (about half of the 30,000 francs cost of making it). His brother inherited the watch after Brunton's death, then sold it to another collector, Murray Marks, who owned around 20 Breguet pieces; Marks sold them all at auction in 1896. There, the Marie Antoinette was bought by Sir David Salomons, at the time the world's expert on Breguet with a personal collection of 124 Breguet items. His daughter inherited some of those, including the No. 160, after Salomons' death in 1925; and either she or her mother donated them all to the new L.A. Mayer Museum for Islamic Art in Jerusalem in 1974.

Museums tend to be the final resting places for the artefacts they display. But this was not the case for the Marie Antoinette. Only nine years later, in 1983, it came to the attention of high-end cat burglar Naaman Diller that the Mayer alarm systems were not working. He was able to enter the building simply by bending back a window bar; and he made off with the museum's entire watch collection, including the Marie Antoinette, valued at the time at $30 million. Diller stashed his haul in safety deposit boxes all around the world, while he waited to find buyers for them. The theft, of the highest value items in Israeli history, went unsolved.

The Swatch group bought the Breguet brand in 1999. Swatch chairman Nicolas G. Hayek mourned the loss to the world of No. 160; and in 2004 Hayek decided to fund a replica. It was an ambitious plan but, only four years later, the reproduction was unveiled at the world's most prestigious watch show, Baselworld 2008. This modern masterpiece was given the Breguet number 1160. Such a watch deserves a presentation case to match. When Hayek heard that Marie Antoinette's favourite oak, growing in the grounds of her favourite palace the Petit Trianon, was going to be felled, he knew at once the wood from which the case should be made. Instead of accepting payment for it, the Versailles estate in which the oak grew invited Hayek to pay for the restoration of a statue. Hayek went further and funded most of the restoration of the Petit Trianon, at a cost of nearly $7.5 million.

Meanwhile, in 2007, Hayek was approached anonymously with an offer to sell him the missing original No. 160. He was able to verify the authenticity of the watch, but refused to compromise himself with an illegal deal. After 24 years, the cold case of the missing watch was revived. Then, in late 2008, a Tel Aviv lawyer contacted the Mayer Museum to say that his client wished to sell back to the museum 40 of the stolen timepieces. His client was Diller's widow Nili Shamrat, to whom he had confessed his crime on his deathbed. The museum willingly paid Ms Shamrat $40,000 and through her was able to unlock Diller's safety deposit boxes in the United States, France, Germany, the Netherlands and Israel. All, including the Marie Antoinette, are now – safely, one hopes – back in the protection of the museum in Jerusalem.

The Marie Antoinette is an extraordinary watch with an extraordinary history. Never seen ticking by the queen for whom it was conceived, nor the count who commissioned it, nor the brilliant craftsman who designed it, it has acquired an aura of beauty and mystery as fine and exciting as Marie Antoinette's reputation – and Breguet's exquisite movement.

American Watch Company Waltham 1857 ('the William Ellery') (1857)

The sale of a Waltham pocket watch for a breath-taking £1.2 million in 2024 briefly returned the forgotten brand to the spotlight. A company frequently overstretched financially nevertheless made its mark in war and peace and was an important player in the process of American industrialization.

Aaron Lufkin Dennison (1812–95), the son of a shoemaker, was apprenticed to a jeweller in Maine, USA. He was fascinated by the movements of the watches that came in for repair and dreamed of making watches himself. He moved to Boston where he worked for the watchmakers Currier & Trott before establishing, in 1844, a company making paper boxes. There he observed at first hand the processes and benefits of mass production. and in 1849, he founded the American Horologe Company, raising $20,000 for the venture with two partners.

Dennison went to England to learn the trade secrets of English watchmakers and found them slow and inefficient. He was determined to apply modern industrial methods to the manufacture of pocket watches. After a succession of name changes – including Warren Manufacturing and the Boston Watch Company – the firm relocated to Waltham, Massachusetts, where it built a factory large enough to accommodate the 90 workers, both Swiss and American, now employed in mass production. Their output was 30 watches a week. Dennison's great innovation was the use of interchangeable parts. Before him, every component of a watch was hand-made, including each individual spring, wheel and screw.

The purchase of the land, the erection of the buildings, the wages of the staff and an economic downturn in 1856 placed too great a strain on the founders' finances and, despite support from the local community, the Boston Watch Company was insolvent by 1857. Its assets were sold off at auction and bought by Royal Robbins, an importer of watches in New York with rather more experience of business than Dennison. He retained Dennison as a superintendent and with new partners set about making the business profitable. In 1859 the company changed its name again, to the American Watch Company.

One of the first models off the production line under the new owners was the Waltham 1857, named the William Ellery. The precise identity of William Ellery is unknown; but the American Watch Company was in the habit of naming models after people and places of significance to the firm; for example, models were named after Robbins and his business partner

An example of the American Watch Company's William Ellery pocket watch, from c. 1879

American tycoon John Jacob Astor IV (1864–1912), photographed c. 1909, three years before the fateful *Titanic* voyage.

The American Watch Company's factory in Waltham, Massachusetts, from an engraving of 1894.

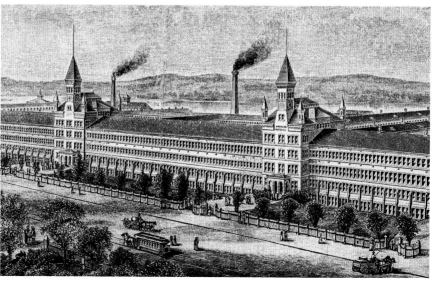

Daniel Appleton, and after Bond Street and Riverside, where the Waltham factory stood.

The William Ellery was a reintroduction of a model produced during Dennison's time at the helm called the C.T. Parker. It sold for $12 (without a case) and was the first American watch to embrace fully the benefits of mass production and interchangeable parts. Robbins oversaw savings through greater efficiency and cost-cutting, but the company continued to struggle as it entered the 1860s, when civil war was about to erupt under the presidency of the newly elected Abraham Lincoln. The American Watch Company was on the brink of bankruptcy.

War, however, proved good for business. The William Ellery, no doubt engraved with declarations of faith, hope and love, proved a popular parting gift to soldiers going off to fight. Soon, it seemed, every soldier wanted to own a William Ellery; sales soared; and by the end of the war in 1865, the Ellery accounted for 40 per cent of the company's sales across five models.

A William Ellery, once the property of a very distinguished person, is now displayed in the National Museum of American History in Washington DC. Following his address in the aftermath of the Battle of Gettysburg, President Lincoln – only two years into his tenancy of the White House – was presented with a Waltham 1857.

The company underwent more changes of name over the following decades, first to the American Waltham Watch Company and then simply the Waltham Watch Company. Its fortunes continued to rise with the expansion of the American railroad network, and it was said that every train company in the US (and many in Europe) ran on Waltham time. Waltham's reputation for accuracy led to the unexpected phenomenon of fakes and copies of Waltham watches being produced in Switzerland in an effort to cash in on its success.

The company hit further financial problems in the crash of 1907, but diversified into car clocks, speedometers, blood pressure gauges and, with the outbreak of World War One, mechanized timer fuses. The war brought another boom in watch sales; but in the Great Depression of the 1920s and 30s, the banks again foreclosed on the company's debts, beginning a long slow process of declining fortunes which ended finally with its dissolution in 1957. The remnants were renamed the Waltham Precision Instruments Company, and the proud company name was licensed to manufacturers of tape recorders and transistor radios. Watches are still produced under the Waltham name but have very little connection with the pioneering business which moved to Massachusetts in 1853.

The Waltham that was bought by a private collector in 2024, not for $12 but for £1.2 million, was a Riverside movement, housed in a solid gold case, engraved with the initials J.J.A. It was first bought, in 1907, by John Jacob Astor IV. He was one of the richest men in the world at the time, and it's a mark of the good reputation of Waltham watches for precision timekeeping that Astor, who could afford to buy any watch, chose to buy a $12 one.

At the time of his death, John Jacob Astor was worth around $87 million (more than $2.75 billion in today's terms). He was, by far, the wealthiest passenger on the luxury liner the RMS *Titanic*, when it sank on its maiden voyage on 15 April 1912. Astor made sure that his wife was safely aboard a lifeboat; but there was no room for him and he went down with the ship. When his body was recovered a week later, they found his Waltham Riverside in his pocket.

The Waltham factory still stands by the riverside, now at the heart of a designated American Waltham Watch Company Historic District in the city. It has been converted into loft apartments.

Cartier Santos (1904)

At the beginning of the twentieth century, fashionable women wore wristwatches. Men, who still formed the majority of the workforce, kept their watches out of harm's way in their waistcoat pockets. But you need a hand to remove a pocket watch; and what do you do if your hands are full?

Time at the start of the century was not yet as precious as it is now. For most men, time was not of the essence. It was counted in hours and minutes, not minutes and seconds. A glance at a pocket watch could happen when it was convenient, without urgency. For some, however, there was never a good moment to drop what you were doing and fumble for a watch. A new breed of men, pilots of aeroplanes, could not afford to take their hands from the controls to consult a watch for important information about, for example, how long they had been flying and how much fuel therefore remained.

Alberto Santos-Dumont was one such pioneer. Heir to a Brazilian coffee fortune, he began his flying career during the balloon age, and was the first man to fly powered airships, which he designed himself. In 1901 he won the Deutsch Prize of 100,000 French francs by taking off from Paris's Parc Saint-Cloud, flying around the Tour Eiffel and landing again

within 30 minutes – his time was 29' 30" – and he was celebrated as the greatest aviator of his day.

Santos-Dumont, who spent most of his time in Paris, then turned his attention to winged aircraft, an altogether more active flying experience. Now he came up against the difficulty of reading a pocket watch while continuing to regulate and steer the contraption in which he sat – again, a craft of his own design. He described the problem to his friend, Louis Cartier, who ran the Paris shop of the expanding Cartier family jewellery and watch business.

The Cartier jewellery brand was founded in Paris in 1847 by Louis-François Cartier. Louis-François's son Alfred succeeded him in 1874 and began to steer the company toward international markets. Alfred's three sons oversaw its triumphant reign as a favourite jeweller of the world's royalty. Britain's King Edward VII ordered 47 tiaras from Cartier for his coronation in 1902, and Cartier also supplied the royal houses of Serbia, Russia, Portugal and Spain. In 1925 it received an order from the Maharajah of Patiala in India worth an unimaginable US$2.75 billion at today's prices.

When Louis Cartier addressed Santos-Dumont's problem, a wristwatch was the obvious solution: the challenge was to design one that was not overtly

A Cartier Santos-Dumont wristwatch made in 1912, only a year after the public launch of the design.

Alberto Santos-Dumont
(1873–1932), demonstrating
the controls of his No. 15
aircraft in 1907.

Cartier's reinvention of the
Santos-Dumont design
included this pair of men's
and women's watches in 1981.

feminine – a man's watch, the first ever man's wristwatch, and the first ever pilot's watch.

Rejecting the smooth regular curves of a woman's watch, Cartier thought in straight lines and defied convention. Clocks and watches were circular, a form dictated by the circular movement of their cogs and hands. But why shouldn't they be square? And so Louis Cartier made his friend a sturdy watch with thick, straight sides – in 1904, the world's first square wristwatch.

The square shape was reinforced with a square inner minute scale, and by the inclining of the bold, straight-lined Roman numerals towards the central point. Cartier's radical design was all the more innovative for appearing in an era when French Art Nouveau was at its height, a world of curvaceous decoration and sinuous forms which drew their inspiration from natural shapes. In focusing on a simple, angled geometric element, Cartier was anticipating the Art Deco movement, which reached its zenith in the 1920s and 30s.

The whole design was a daring departure, one most suitable for an adventurer of the skies such as Santos-Dumont. His escapades in airships of his own design, including his Eiffel Tower triumph, had made him a European celebrity. His No. 6 balloon toured the continent; and when he turned his attention to aeroplanes, he became the first pilot to be filmed in flight. His No. 19 monoplane was the first aircraft to be commercially mass-produced, both as a flight-ready machine and in kit form.

Whenever Santos-Dumont flew, and at his many public engagements, he wore Cartier's distinctive watch on his wrist. Its simple elegance and unusual form attracted attention and created a demand. After many requests for copies of the one-off creation,

Louis Cartier relented and launched a mass-produced version of it in 1911, using a movement designed in collaboration with Jaeger of Switzerland. All its hallmarks were in place from the start – the square face, the visible screws on the bezel, the blue sapphire on the crown – and they all remain essential elements of the Cartier Santos's design, well over a century later. Today it is available in some 66 variations of size, precious metal and function, ranging in price from a positively affordable £3,750 to £65,000.

Santos-Dumont is a national hero in Brazil, where his contributions to aviation are considered to be greater than those even of the Wright brothers. His monoplanes were used to train pilots during World War One, but he was horrified by the development of aerial warfare and campaigned against it for the rest of his life. In despair he eventually burned all his diaries and papers, and his physical health declined. He saw aerial warfare again in 1932 when planes played a part in a civil war in Brazil. 'My God! My God!,' he wrote, 'Is there no way to avoid the bloodshed of brothers? Why did I make this invention which, instead of contributing to the love between men, turns into a cursed weapon of war?' He committed suicide in July that year.

The watch that Louis Cartier made for his friend Alberto is lost, but some examples of the earliest production runs have survived. The Santos single-handedly created a fashion for uncircular watches and even when, with the waning of the Art Deco movement, public demand for such things declined, the Santos remained a watch of style and statement for the discerning wrist. Furthermore, its early success laid the ground for another iconic Cartier watch – the beautiful but inelegantly named Tank.

'Whenever Santos-Dumont flew, and at his many public engagements, he wore Cartier's distinctive watch on his wrist. Its simple elegance and unusual form attracted attention and created a demand.'

Cartier Tank (1919)

A distinctively shaped luxury watch seems a million miles away from the ugly World War One fighting machine that inspired it. Launched as the old world order was about to disappear forever, it gave high society a sense of continuity and carefree wealth.

The Cartier Tank wristwatch has its roots in an earlier Cartier watch, designed by Louis Cartier in 1904. Louis ran the Paris branch of Cartier, and had a reputation for creating colourful jewellery, so-called mystery clocks (which had transparent dials through which no mechanism was visible) and ladies' wristwatches. Men, as a rule, carried pocket watches. When his friend, the pilot Alberto Santos-Dumont, bemoaned the lack of a gentleman's watch that he could consult without taking his hands off the controls of his aeroplane, Louis Cartier delivered, in an age of circular dials, an eye-catching square wristwatch.

The Cartier Santos went into production in 1911 and has remained a staple of the Cartier house ever since. In 1916 France was under sustained attack from Germany along its border – the battle of Verdun raged for more than 10 months that year. The war never reached Paris, but its sounds and sights were well reported in the nation's capital.

From such a grim aspect of humanity came Louis's inspiration for a new watch design.

It takes an inventive mind to see a wristwatch in an armoured tank. The tank in question was, naturally, a French one. Tanks were in their infancy, and the Renault FT-17 was the first to incorporate a fully rotating turret. It also differed from the early British rhomboid profile; the Renault's caterpillar tracks were of necessity housed below the turret, low in the overall shape, and looking more like the familiar modern image of a tank. The tracks extended beyond and behind the tank's cabin, and in Louis Cartier's imagination the plan of the Renault FT-17 resembled nothing so much as a giant watch, a Santos watch. The cabin was the face; the turret represented the turning hands; and the tracks running from fore to aft could be seen as the lugs to which to attach a watchstrap.

Thus the Cartier Tank was born. The broad protective straight lines of its bezel framed a delicate rectangular dial, like a stretched version of the Santos, with a fine railroad-style minute scale that echoed the segments of a caterpillar track. There was another warfare allusion in Cartier's design: when the line of the sides of the bezel is extended to form the strap lugs, it is known as a *brancard* – the French word for a medical stretcher for carrying the injured to safety. During that terrible war

A Cartier Tank made in 1962 in 18ct gold, which once belonged to Jacqueline Kennedy Onassis (1929–94).

Rudolph Valentino (1895–1926) wearing an anachronistic wristwatch in his final film *The Son of the Sheik* (1926) opposite Vilma Bánky (1901–91).

A convoy of Renault FT-17 tanks in the Aisne region of France, photographed in 1918, the year the Cartier Tank watch was first launched, before entering full production a year later.

Europeans on all sides were only too familiar with the form of a stretcher.

Perhaps it was its references to the continuing conflict which divided critics when it first appeared in 1918. When it went into production the following year it had a very limited run: only six were made. Louis presented one of the prototypes to the US Army general John Pershing, who commanded the US American Expeditionary Force (AEF) from the US's entry into World War One in 1917 until its withdrawal from Europe in 1920.

Pershing was greatly admired for leading the US troops whose arrival in Europe eventually turned the tide decisively in the Allies' favour. Although some of his tactics of direct assault are now considered costly and unwise, his long experience in earlier conflicts gave him a great understanding of life on the front line. In response to the blight of trench foot, which affected many of the infantry, he designed new footwear, today called the Pershing boot. Although he resisted the full assimilation of the US troops into the French Army – US racial policy forbade the participation of America's 'separate but equal' African American units in the AEF – Pershing is notable too for allowing those units to fight under French command.

World War One played an important role in expanding the use of wristwatches by men. Synchronized attacks depended on synchronized watches. And just as Alberto Santos-Dumont had needed a timepiece that he could consult without using his hands, so soldiers could not afford to remove their hands from rifles and cannons which they had to be ready to fire at the appointed hour. After the war the habit of wearing watches continued and the Tank began to be recognized as a classic of design. More than the Santos before it, the Tank introduced the wristwatch as fashion accessory, not merely as timepiece.

It was in that sense very much of its time, an age of style when many of the greats of haute couture first emerged. The era oversaw the establishment of cinema as a form of entertainment and witnessed the beginnings of the public's obsession with celebrity and personality. The world now had stars – not only movie stars but musicians, sportsmen and women, and even those who were admired simply for being glamorous rather than accomplishing any remarkable achievements.

Among those happy to be seen wearing a Cartier Tank were the film actors Rudolph Valentino, Gary Cooper, Clark Gable, Stewart Granger and the great style icon of the 1960s, Steve McQueen. Bandleaders of very different musical genres, Duke Ellington and Patti Smith, both sported a Tank on their wrists. Author Truman Capote and boxing champion Muhammad Ali favoured the Tank in one of its many incarnations. Actresses Tallulah Bankhead and Ingrid Bergman were fans, as were Princess Diana and the most glamorous of first ladies, Jacqueline Kennedy Onassis and Michelle Obama. Fashion designer Ralph Lauren chose to wear a Tank.

The Cartier Tank became for many 'The Watch To Be Seen Wearing', and no one exemplified this more than the New York pop artist Andy Warhol, whose many claims to fame include his remark: 'I don't wear a Tank to tell the time. In fact, I never wind it. I wear a Tank because it's the watch to wear.' To Warhol is also attributed the remark: 'In the future, everyone will be world-famous for fifteen minutes.' If that's true, what better way to measure those 15 minutes than with a Cartier Tank?

'It takes an inventive mind to see a wristwatch in an armoured tank ... The cabin was the face; the turret represented the turning hands; and the tracks running from fore to aft could be seen as the lugs to which to attach a watchstrap.'

Rolex Oyster (1926)

The Rolex Oyster wasn't the first watch to claim to be waterproof, but it was the first to justify the claim. It was the first watch to be actively marketed through celebrity endorsements too; and who better to endorse a waterproof watch than a cross-channel swimmer?

Water is the enemy of the watch. Condensation inside the crystal makes it impossible to read and rust inside the movement brings the whole mechanism to a standstill. Since the nineteenth century watchmakers had sought solutions to this problem. A Swiss maker of watch cases, François Borgel devised innovative one-piece and three-piece case designs which attached the movement to the shell by means of a threaded ring instead of individual screws. Rolex experimented with both in the early twentieth century to produce water-resistant wristwatches. In particular, one, known as the Hermetic, developed into the Rolex Submariner (see page 74).

The weakest point in any watch, in terms of water ingress, is the crown, a problem which another Swiss pair, Paul Perregaux and Georges Perret took on. Although their counter-threaded solution was flawed, it is no coincidence that Rolex bought their patent for the design on 24 July 1926 and registered the Oyster trademark only five days later. Rolex could see the potential in the Perregaux–Perret crown, whose failing was that without a clutch (the click when you push the winder back in) it could not be fully closed when fully wound. When the first iteration of the Rolex Oyster appeared later in 1926, it introduced a clutched crown and an octagonal version by C.R. Spillmann & Co of Borgel's three-piece case.

It's all very well to claim to be waterproof, but Rolex knew that a sceptical public demands evidence. An opportunity presented itself late in 1927. Mercedes Gleitze was a British swimmer who built a successful career by establishing and breaking swimming records. Her 10 hours 45 minutes swim in the River Thames in 1923 was an endurance record for a woman at the time; and she became the first British woman to swim across the English Channel on 7 October 1927, her eighth attempt at the feat. Her triumph was undermined, however, when a London gynaecologist, Dr Dorothy Cochrane Logan, claimed to have swum it in a faster time on 10 October. Dr Logan really had made several (unsuccessful) attempts, but on this occasion she had made most of the crossing by boat. She perpetrated the hoax to expose the lack of rigorous authentication of cross-channel swims. However, the damage to Gleitze's claim had been done.

The distinctive octagonal case of the Rolex Oyster as launched in 1926.

Above: British swimmer
Mercedes Gleitze (1901–81)
and her support team, about
to abandon her Vindication
cross-channel attempt only
eight miles short of Dover on
21 October 1927.

Left: Tennis player Roger
Federer shows off his Rolex
Oyster as he holds the Men's
Singles trophy at Wimbledon
on 5 July 2009, beating
Pete Sampras's record
of Grand Slam wins.

The press got hold of the story and urged Gleitze to undertake a repeat performance, a so-called Vindication Swim, to restore her reputation. Gleitze reluctantly agreed, although the swim would inevitably take place later in the year when water conditions were really too rough and cold for an attempt. Rolex seized the moment and sponsored Gleitze to wear an Oyster around her neck for the challenge.

After more than 10 hours in the water, Gleitze was unable to complete the Vindication Swim; but her endurance of the chilling conditions persuaded the press and the public that her earlier claim was genuine. The publicity surrounding Logan's hoax was the making of Gleitze's reputation and career and she went on to break records all around the world, including swimming all the way round the 100-mile coastline of the Isle of Man, and becoming the first person to swim from Europe to Africa across the Strait of Gibraltar, and to Robben Island and back from Cape Town.

The sponsorship which she now attracted – from makers of bathing caps, honey, corsets, Irish whiskey and English tea among others – enabled her to open several Mercedes Gleitze Homes for the homeless in England. A biographical film, *Vindication Swim*, was released in 2024.

The Oyster around Gleitze's neck survived her ordeal without admitting any seawater, providing Rolex with a vindication of its own. Gleitze became an ambassador for the brand for the rest of her life, and her image is still used by the watchmaker today. As a demonstration of waterproofing, Gleitze's swim was indisputable and ensured the best possible launch for the Rolex Oyster.

It also proved the value of celebrity endorsement, to both parties. Throughout the Oyster's life, Rolex advertising associated it with endeavours that reflected a spirit of human achievement whenever possible. An Oyster was fixed to the outside of a plane which flew over Mount Everest in 1933, demonstrating its resilience in extremes of altitude, air pressure and temperature. The stunt was so successful that Rolex returned to the world's highest mountain in 1953, when the expedition which finally conquered it used Oysters. In the same year, Rolex Oysters were the official watch of Pan Am Airlines when it introduced transcontinental flights across time zones at the dawn of the jet age.

Rolex found a new face and wrist for the Oyster in 1935 when Malcolm Campbell wore one in his successful 300mph (483kmh) assault on the world's land speed record. Campbell did so without any financial benefit from sponsorship, a fact which Rolex eagerly cited in advertisements to increase the authenticity of Campbell's endorsement.

The Oyster secured Rolex's reputation, and Mercedes Gleitze secured the Oyster's. Since 1927 the rich and famous have helped to preserve it. World leaders from Winston Churchill through JFK and Martin Luther King Jr to Barack Obama have all owned versions of the Oyster family, although Kennedy is said never to have worn his – it was a gift from Marilyn Monroe on the occasion at which she famously and breathlessly sang 'Happy Birthday' to him, and was inscribed 'Jack, with love as always, Marilyn'. Jack was a married man, and it might have been unwise to flaunt such a gift from a woman with whom he was having an affair.

Churchill's was a gift from Rolex in 1947, the 100,000th watch which the company had produced in its history. President Dwight Eisenhower received the 150,000th, an Oyster Datejust. Film star and amateur motor racing enthusiast Paul Newman famously wore an Oyster Daytona, named after the Florida racetrack. Tennis player Roger Federer, a long-time brand ambassador, wore a Rolex Oyster Perpetual Datejust II when he overtook Pete Sampras's record of Grand Slam wins at Wimbledon in 2009.

Longines Lindbergh Hour Angle (1931)

In the days before the precision of satellite-driven Global Positioning Systems (GPS), navigation in the air was the same complicated mathematical process that it was at sea, involving sextants, observation of the stars and the undivided attention of a navigation officer, a luxury a solo flyer was denied.

Charles Lindbergh was a relatively inexperienced pilot in a somewhat flimsy aircraft, the *Spirit of St Louis*, when he became the first man to fly solo across the Atlantic Ocean in 1927 in his Ryan monoplane. He navigated by dead reckoning – that is, he measured the distance between Paris and New York on a map, pointed his plane in the right direction with the aid of a compass, and then estimated his position based on his airspeed and the length of time he had been travelling.

Lindbergh was lucky: the wind, the weather and the air pressure remained constant and favourable, when changes in either could have thrown him wildly off course. Six men who had previously tried an Atlantic crossing had died in the attempt and, on a later flight from Cuba to Florida, Lindbergh got into no small degree of trouble using the same techniques. He therefore sought the wisdom of the acknowledged master of navigation in his day, Lieutenant Commander Philip Van Horn Weems of the US Navy.

Weems was developing a new system of aeronautical navigation. At any given moment, every star is directly overhead somewhere on Earth. That position, called its 'geographical point', changes with the rotation of the Earth, and the stars' points trace out a circle around the Earth's surface, its 'circle of position'. By measuring the direction of the star with a compass, and its angle of elevation with a sextant, one can determine one's own position in relation to the star's geographical point.

These are the complex set of interrelated variables involved in calculating one's position. For real accuracy, observations of two separate celestial objects had to be recorded and cross referenced, a time-consuming exercise which was acceptable on board a slow-moving ship but not in the air where miles flew by quickly. For a pilot flying solo it was impossible.

Weems was determined to simplify the process of establishing one's latitude and longitude. Latitude could be approximately gauged, at least in the Northern Hemisphere, by the elevation of the star Polaris above the northern horizon. Longitude had long been harder to assess, until clockmaker James Harrison solved the problem. With one watch set to Greenwich Mean Time and another to local time, one can know how far East or West of Greenwich one

The Longines Lindbergh Hour Angle watch owned by aviation pioneer Charles Lindbergh (1902–74).

After his ground-breaking transatlantic crossing on 21–22 May 1927, Charles Lindbergh flies over Paris in his plane *Spirit of St Louis*.

The Weems Second Setting watch, predecessor of the Lindbergh Hour Angle, which could be synchronized to the second with Greenwich Mean Time.

is, and therefore one's longitude – the Earth revolves 15° in one hour.

Weems's system brought all these elements together. He compiled an almanac which gave the geographical points and circles of position of the Sun, Moon and important navigational stars throughout the year. He worked with watchmaker Longines to produce a timepiece that could be synchronized to the second with Greenwich Mean Time. Without that precision, watches could only be accurate to within one minute, this at airspeeds when even one second can take you far off course. Weems also introduced an inner scale on the watch face which was divided not into 12 hours or 60 seconds but 15, making easier the calculation of the 'equation of time', the effect of time difference between Greenwich and local.

Weems and Charles Lindbergh worked together on refining the system, and one of Lindbergh's biggest contributions was to the watch. He suggested a rotating bezel, again divided into 15 'hours' and their quarters, in effect turning the watch into a circular slide rule by which the equation of time could be quickly calculated. The man to whom he took his suggestion was John Heinmuller, a fellow pilot and an executive at Longines, who had been the official timer when Lindbergh completed his record-breaking transatlantic flight in Paris.

The Longines Weems Second Setting watch was duly succeeded by the Longines Lindbergh Hour Angle watch in 1931 – 'hour angle' being the navigational term for the 15° of longitude through which the Earth turned in an hour. It had a large case, 47.5mm in diameter, and an outsize crown so that it could be wound with gloves on. As Lindbergh wrote in a letter to Heinmuller after receiving the prototype Hour Angle watch: 'The arrangement seems excellent and I believe will save a number of seconds in obtaining a position and also simplify the procedure to some extent.'

Between them Weems and Lindbergh revolutionized aerial navigation, or avigation as it came to be called. Lindbergh became a global celebrity after his triumphant crossing – he circled the Eiffel Tower before touching down at Le Bourget airport, on the outskirts of Paris, where a souvenir-hungry mob stripped the *Spirit of St Louis* of everything that could be removed and even began cutting off ribbons of the linen which coated the plane's frame, before an armed guard with fixed bayonets protected it from further damage.

Tragedy struck the Lindbergh family only a year after the launch of the Hour Angle watch. Lindbergh's son was kidnapped and killed in the spring of 1932. His fame and the sensational reporting of the crime and subsequent trial drove the family into hiding in Europe, from where they returned to the US in 1939. Charles Lindbergh's views on Jews and US neutrality persuaded the American public that he was a Nazi sympathizer (something he never expressed) and his application to join the US Air Force after Pearl Harbor was denied by President Roosevelt himself.

Lindbergh's personal Hour Angle watch now sits in the Smithsonian National Air and Space Museum in Washington DC. Few of the original Hour Angles survive, but Longines has periodically released faithful facsimiles – first in 1987 and several times since. A 2027 centenary celebration of Lindbergh's achievement seems inevitable. Weems' standard text *Air Navigation*, in a 1941 edition, is available online as a free download and instruction manual for the watch's use. Readers wishing to follow in Lindbergh's illustrious vapour trails can therefore do so: armed with those two pieces of equipment, the watch and the manual, all you need is a small biplane and a spare 33½ hours – the time it took Lindbergh to fly from New York to Paris. Then again, since Lindbergh achieved it by dead reckoning, surely the use of any navigational aids, even his own, would be cheating?

Jaeger-LeCoultre Reverso (1931)

An idea born on the playing fields of British colonial India found expression in a masterpiece of Swiss engineering and Art Deco styling. As if its own inherent beauty were not enough, the Reverso also offered watch-wearers a blank canvas for their own imaginations.

Jaeger-LeCoultre watch movements have been a by-word for excellence since the early nineteenth century when the LeCoultre family founded the village of Le Sentier in Switzerland's Vallée de Joux and began making movements there. By 1903, when French watchmaker Edmond Jaeger asked LeCoultre to produce his revolutionary new super-thin movement design, the company employed 500 people at the factory in Le Sentier where it is still made today. Jaeger-LeCoultre supplied movements to many of the biggest watchmakers of the time, including Patek Philippe.

Time and time again, the firm made landmark innovations in watch-building. Antoine LeCoultre invented the machinery for producing watch pinions – the gear wheels that turn the hands, and which previously had to be painstakingly handmade – in 1833. Eleven years later he came up with the *Millionomètre*, a device capable of measuring parts to an accuracy of one micron (one thousandth of a millimetre, or one millionth of a metre). Three years after that he devised a keyless winding system which combined the function with that of adjusting the hands, in a single knob, the crown; before then pocket watches had to be wound with a small key, usually inserted into the back.

LeCoultre & Co again broke new ground in 1866 by adding complications to their redoubtable movements – functions beyond the mere telling of time such as calendars, chronographs and repeaters, all run by the same pocketwatch movement. The LeCoultre Calibre 145, introduced in 1907, remains the thinnest movement ever produced, shallower than a coin at only 1.38mm (0.054in). The company's capacity for elegant, precise micro-engineering was unrivalled.

Meanwhile in India, in 1931, two teams of British army officers were competing in a game of polo – a sport in which players on horseback wield long-handled mallets attempting to drive a white ball (similar in size to a cricket ball) on the ground into their opponents' goal. It's an energetic, physical game with a high risk of rough contact between any combination of players, horses, mallets and ball. Little wonder that after this particular match, a player complained to one of the spectators that the glass on his watch had been smashed.

A Jaeger-LeCoultre Reverso from c. 1940.

A 1996 limited edition of the Jaeger-LeCoultre Reverso, reversed to show *Summer*, an enamel design in the style of Alphonse Mucha's 1896 series *The Seasons*.

The same watch turned to show the watch face – note the crown, now on the right of the dial.

By chance the spectator was César de Trey, a Swiss collector of watches. Trey had the ear of Jacques-Davide LeCoultre and put the problem to him. LeCoultre passed it on to the designers at Jaeger, who in their turn approached René-Alfred Chauvot, a French Art Deco artist and engineer. It was Chauvot who delivered the elegant solution to the polo player's problem: the defining characteristic of the Reverso, a rectangular watch which slides sideways in its mount so that it can be flipped back into place face down, offering only the metal back of the watch to the violent attentions of other polo players.

The quadrilateral shape was perfectly, geometrically Art Deco, emphasized by the parallel lines above and below the face, and the railtrack-style minute scale around the edge of the face. When a sub-dial counting seconds was added at 6 o'clock in 1934, it just had to be a square.

Almost accidentally, that bare back panel became the Reverso's greatest asset – not as protective armour for the face, but as a blank canvas. Here was a private space, normally hidden, to be engraved or enamelled at the whim of each watch's owner. Jaeger-LeCoultre offered the service by making its staff engravers available to its clients; and it also issued special edition Reversos to commemorate some events. For example, in 1933 the Balbo Reverso celebrated the transatlantic expedition that year by a flotilla of 24 seaplanes led by the Italian Secretary of State for the Air, Italo Balbo. The watches were decorated with a map of the Atlantic showing the eight legs between Rome and Chicago which Balbo followed. A similar decoration in 1935 mapped the ground-breaking non-stop flight which Amelia Earhart made from Mexico to Newark, New Jersey.

Some people used the space to declare their ownership. General Douglas MacArthur, who spearheaded the American war effort in the Pacific, had his Reverso engraved with a stylish black-laquered monogram, 'D Mac A'. The Reverso of King Edward VIII of Great Britain is a lesson in taking a moment before committing. It was engraved with his name, a crown and the year 1937: but unfortunately, by 1937, he had already abdicated the throne.

Others chose pictures over words. One watch was graced with an enamel painting of Rama, a Hindu god whose life is traditionally used to illustrate social rights and responsibilities. The watch in question was decorated in 1949, only two years after India won its independence from polo-playing Britain, when Indian society was most keenly aware of moral duty and fairness. Nearly 50 years later, Hungarian watchmaker Miklos Merczel set up a fully-fledged enamel department at Jaeger-LeCoultre. It announced its existence in 1996 with a stunning limited edition of reproductions of Alphonse Mucha's Art Nouveau series *The Seasons*. Tributes to other artists have followed, including Hokusai and Van Gogh.

The best known and most intriguing Reverso enamel dates from early in the brand's history and represents another Indian connection. One Reverso manufactured in 1936 is known as the Indian Beauty, after the elegant and well-dressed woman in the portrait on its back. Much admired by collectors, the identity of the sitter remained unknown for many years. Recent detective work has identified a possible subject, however. When the Maharajah of Tripura, a state in northeastern India, died in 1947, his son and heir was only 14 years old; and so the Maharajah's widow, the boy's mother, ruled as regent for the next two years. Based on the portrait's hairstyle, pose and clothing, it is likely that she, the Maharani Kanchan Prabha Devi of Tripura, is the Indian Beauty in question; and perhaps the watch was a gift from her, or maybe to her son, as a reminder of her role in his and Tripura's life.

The Reverso, that most cleverly engineered of watches, has been a vehicle for many complications over the decades, with the addition of more functions and more faces – sometimes double-sided, sometimes unfolding to reveal three distinct dials. The need for protection which first drove its creation has made it a favourite with Hollywood action heroes: Matt Damon (Jason Bourne) and Pierce Brosnan (James Bond) are among its modern-day devotees.

Ingersoll Mickey Mouse (1933)

Not all iconic watches are aimed at the luxury market. In 1957 the animator Walt Disney was presented with the 25 millionth Mickey Mouse watch. One of the most popular watches of all time, a Mickey Mouse timepiece is affordably collectable in most of the many guises of its ninety years.

The history of Mickey Mouse is well known. The animated character first appeared in public in Walt Disney's short film *Steamboat Willie* in 1928. The eight-minute masterpiece secured the reputations of both Disney and his star; but as recession and depression gripped northern America, cinema-going became a luxury few could afford. Disney feared for the financial future of his young animation studio. In an effort to raise funds, he hired Herman Kamen, a former hat salesman, to develop the licensing and merchandizing side of the business.

Kamen was incredibly good at his job and placed Mickey on everything from breakfast cereal packs to toothpaste tubes. He persuaded watchmakers Ingersoll-Westbury to produce a range of Mickey Mouse timepieces – a pocket watch, a mantelpiece clock, an electric clock, and of course, a wristwatch – and launched them at the Chicago Century of Progress Exposition in 1933. Retailers placed huge orders, and on the first day that the watches went on sale in Macy's in New York, the department store sold 11,000 of them, at $3.25 each. In Britain the watch was priced at 15 shillings (just under £67 in 2024).

Ingersoll-Westbury had the inspired idea of using Mickey's big-gloved hands as the hands of the watch – he was after all an animated character. Mickey's public debut *Steamboat Willie* was in black and white, and he didn't appear in full Technicolor until 1935, two years after the launch of the Mickey Mouse watch. Although Mickey's signature gloves have always been white on film, Ingersoll coloured them yellow.

The company continued to produce the watches for the next 40 years. The first generation of watches had the added feature of a sub-dial at 6 o'clock showing the seconds by means of three tiny Mickeys chasing each other in a circle. The strap was metal, pierced to reveal Mickey's profile. The first changes came in 1937. What had previously been a unisex item appeared in boys' and girls' versions (the latter with a thinner strap). The dial, originally circular, was now barrel shaped with bowed sides and straight top and bottom – and in 1938 it went full Tank as a pure rectangle. The chasing Mickeys were replaced by a simple pointer in the second sub-dial.

Two original-edition Mickey Mouse watches, launched by Ingersoll-Westbury at the Chicago Century of Progress Exposition in 1933 – the lower one has the metal strap stamped through with the classic Mickey Mouse profile.

Seiko's take on the Mickey Mouse watch, with a quartz movement, from the 1980s.

An Ingersoll advertisement from *Life* magazine promoting Mickey Mouse watches, pens and alarm clocks as presents for Christmas 1948.

By 1942, the year in which Ingersoll was bought by US Time, the sub-dial had gone altogether, although otherwise US Time was not about to change a winning formula – it even retained the Ingersoll name on the face. One particularly rare version appeared in 1948 – a circular dial in which Mickey's hands were luminous. The radium used to make them glow was highly poisonous to the watchmakers whose job it was to paint each glove by hand and the practice has long since ceased. But commentators are quick to reassure collectors that luminous Mickeys are within safe levels.

After 25 million sales, public interest in the Mickey Mouse watch may have tailed off. A half-hearted attempt to refresh the brand came in the 1950s when the numbers, which had always been black, became red. In a surprisingly minimalist move during the 1960s, US Time removed the image of Mickey from the dial completely, leaving only his name in matching red. The company stopped making Mickey Mouse watches altogether in 1971.

All these variations are collectable; and because the watches were produced in such vast numbers, they are relatively inexpensive and easy to find and date. The end of US Time production (latterly under the name Timex) did not mean that Mickey Mouse himself was out of time. Quartz movement innovators Seiko acquired the rights to the character and released several designs under its brands Seiko, Pulsar and Lorus. Some, such as the Seiko model featuring both Mickey and Minnie Mouse, were made in limited editions of 500. One of the rarest is a Lorus version which plays music.

Seiko's interest and its limited editions are indicative of a change in status for the watch. No longer a novelty item, the Mickey Mouse watch has been around long enough to be a design and style icon; and as such, eligible for some prestigious makeovers. Swatch issued a series of two Mickey Mouse wristwatches in 2018, designed by the *enfant terrible* of modern British art, Damien Hirst, who reduced Mickey to a stylish set of black, white, red and yellow circles to celebrate *Steamboat Willie*'s 90th birthday. The larger watch, on a mirrored background, was limited to an edition of 19,999, the smaller, on black, to 1,999. They were all sold on Swatch's website within a period of 24 hours; a set of both sizes was sold at Christie's auction house the following year for US$4,375.

Mickey has also attracted the attention of one of the greatest watchmakers of all time, Gérald Genta. Genta established his credentials by designing Patek Philippe's Nautilus, the Audemars Piguet Royal Oak and Cartier's Pasha de Cartier. He has been described by Christie's as the Fabergé of watchmakers. His one-off creations for fabulously wealthy clients, including the royal families of Europe and northern Africa, often took five years to make.

Genta acquired special licensing rights from the Walt Disney Company in the early 1980s and launched a collection of watches in 1988 bearing the likenesses of Donald Duck, Goofy, Scrooge McDuck, Minnie Mouse and of course Mickey, selling for between $3,000 and $4,000.

This amounted to a bargain price for a Genta watch. The Octa Grande Sonnerie Tourbillon, produced for his own company, contained four bells and rang out with the same quarterly chimes as London's Big Ben – at a price of $810,200. His Grande Sonnerie Retro, launched in 1994 to mark the 25th anniversary of the founding of his brand, had 800 moving parts and eight sub-dials within its face. It was at the time the most complicated watch in history, with a price tag to match: $2,000,000. Strictly speaking each copy was a one-off, and Christie's sold one in a platinum case with a mother-of-pearl dial at auction in 2021 for a mere $500,000. The low price reflected the fact that the watch's movement was non-functioning, and Genta (who died in 2011) was not available to repair it.

Genta's Disney watches made their debut in sensational fashion at Baselworld, the annual showcase for Swiss and international watchmakers. When the organizers saw cartoon characters on display on Genta's stand, his reputation counted for nothing. In a red mist of horological snobbery they ordered him to remove the offending watches, which they thought lowered the tone of the event. Genta, incensed by their attitude, removed not only his Disney collection, but himself and his entire contribution to that year's event, and stormed out of the building.

Gérald Genta was notable for not wearing a watch. He liked to make them, but not to wear them.

Panerai Radiomir (1935)

One of the world's most iconic watches was a closely guarded 'official secret' for the first 58 years of its life. When it finally went public in 1993, the rugged Panerai Radiomir had nothing to prove, having been the watch of choice for elite Italian naval forces. This is not a watch to be worn just for show.

Giovanni Panerai opened a shop in Florence, Italy, in 1860. He sold Swiss watches; but since the watches arrived from Switzerland unassembled, he set up a small workshop and learned in the best way – hands-on – what makes watches tick. By the turn of the century his grandson Guido was running the business.

Across the Adriatic Sea, political tensions were growing in the Balkan states that would eventually explode into World War One. Guido Panerai saw an emerging market for precision devices: military compasses, depth gauges and the like. He devised, and in 1916 patented, a powder whose ingredients included the new miracle element radium, discovered only 18 years earlier by Pierre and Marie Curie. The powder – which Panerai named Radiomir – emitted light, and Panerai had first used it the previous year within an illuminated gun sight of his own invention.

We know now that radium is a toxic element with numerous health risks. But at the time, the advantage of being able to see one's instruments in the dark, whether at night or in the unlit depths of the sea, was not lost on the Royal Italian Navy, which began to buy equipment manufactured or modified by Panerai. The navy, established a year after Giovanni Panerai opened his shop in Florence, played a significant role during World War One by confining the Austro-Hungarian surface fleet to the Adriatic Sea, but it was unable to restrict the movement of the enemy's submarines and suffered substantial losses. It was, however, able to develop its small-scale naval activities, thanks in no small part to its Panerai instruments. In one notable engagement, two Italian officers – Raffaele Paolucci and Raffaele Rossetti – slipped into the Croatian port of Pola on a manned torpedo and sank the Austro-Hungarian flagship SMS *Viribus Unitis*, after warning the Pola commander to try to save fellow seamen's lives. They were unaware that the war had ended and that the ship was now the flagship of the Yugoslavian navy, a gift from Austro-Hungary now renamed the *Jugoslavija*. Nevertheless, it was a military success, made possible by Panerai instruments including the timers on the mines which sank the ship; and the two seamen were awarded the Gold Medal of Military Valour of the then-Kingdom of Italy. So bright was the radiomir that some divers took to wrapping seaweed around their wrists to conceal the light from enemy eyes.

A very rare Panerai prototype, the Radiomir SLC, from 1935 – SLC stood for Siluro a Lento Corsa, 'slow-moving torpedo', and only two are known to exist.

Marie and Pierre Curie, discoverers of radium (the luminous ingredient of radiomir), in their Paris laboratory in 1896.

SMS *Viribus Unitis*, the flgship of the Austro-Hungarian navy, during sea trials in the Adriatic in 1912 – it was sunk by Italian divers wearing Radiomir wristwatches in 1918.

After the war Italy set about rebuilding its navy, partly to replace its Adriatic losses and partly because, with the rise of Italian fascism, it felt imprisoned by the British Royal Navy. Britain controlled both entrances to the Mediterranean Sea – the Straits of Gibraltar in the west and the Suez Canal in the east. As part of this naval expansion, the navy commissioned Panerai to produce a watch suitable for a new programme of covert underwater activities involving divers and submersible vehicles. Of the many prototypes that Panerai developed in the course of 1935, No. 2533 was the most successful, using a Rolex movement adapted and encased by Panerai. With further modifications, as No. 3646, it went into production. The result was the Panerai Radiomir, named after the substance that provided one of its distinguishing features, and it was released to the Royal Italian Navy in 1936.

The Radiomir had from the start its distinctive cushion shape, a square with bowed sides; and its large (47mm) minimal display was intended to make consulting it under pressure as clear and unconfusing as possible. The dial was a radiomir sandwich: a lower plate covered in the luminous paste was covered by an upper face of anodized aluminium, from which the indices were cut out. These perforations allowed the radiomir to shine through more sharply and distinctly than hand-painted numbers would. The hours were all simple lines or batons except for the 3, 6, 9 and 12. The waterproof leather strap was extra-long so that it would fit around a bulky diving suit.

Panerai continued to adapt the watch as ideas presented themselves. In 1940, with World War Two underway, Panerai changed the case, also made by Rolex, to one constructed from a single piece of stainless steel, improving its ability to withstand water pressure.

The watch saw plenty of action during the war. A group of Italian commandos led by Lieutenant Luigi Durand De La Penne pulled off a spectacular raid on the British Mediterranean fleet stationed in Alexandria in late 1941. Arriving underwater on updated versions of the manned torpedo which had worked so well in 1918, they disabled three British ships – a tanker and two battleships. Penne and his right-hand man were captured and in a spirit of gentlemanly conduct, as Paolucci and Rossetti had done, warned the local commandant of the mines they had placed. They were promptly imprisoned in the hold of one of the ships; but they survived the explosion and the British officer in question, impressed by the boldness and success of the attack, took the remarkable step of recommending

Penne for the Italian Gold Medal of Military Valour (the same award that Paolucci and Rossetti had received), for delivering 'the greatest blow that a single man has ever inflicted on a fleet'.

War was ultimately not good for the Italian navy. Having allied itself with Nazi Germany, it was decimated. Panerai Radiomir watches taken as trophies were the first indication to the world outside Italy that such a timepiece existed. In the wake of the atomic bombs which ended the war in Japan, the dangers of radium became more widely understood, and Panerai developed luminor, a tritium-based compound, as a replacement for radiomir. Its Luminor watches, launched in 1950, introduced a new feature – a protective bridge over the crown that eliminated its vulnerability in the undersea world of espionage and sabotage.

Panerai continued to supply the Italian Navy (no longer royal since the abolition of the Italian monarchy at the end of the war) as the pre-eminent maker of diving watches, wrist-worn depth gauges and other equipment. Its reputation grew, and during the Suez crisis of 1956, the Egyptian Navy commissioned a new, giant version of the watch as it fought with Israel, France and Britain for control of the Suez Canal. The dial of this version, known to this day as l'Egiziano, 'the Egyptian', was a full 60mm in diameter. It could function in depths of 200m (656ft), and boasted an eight-day movement, a useful attribute on covert missions which might last several days and nights.

By the 1970s Panerai watches were struggling to meet the navy's specifications. With the death of Giuseppe Panerai in 1972 the company passed out of the family to Dino Zei, a retired Italian navy colonel who had been responsible for the navy's procurement of Panerai instruments. Zei's tenure ensured the navy's custom for a few more years; but in 1993 he oversaw the company's first public-facing production in its nearly 60-year history, a range of models inspired by the company's role in World War Two. Among those who pounced on this new arrival on the world stage was Sylvester Stallone, whose film roles such as Rambo made him a good fit for the brand. He wore one prominently in his 1996 film *Daylight*. The resulting exposure completed the brand's transition from 'official secret' to luxury object of desire. In 1997 Panerai ceased all military production and planned a series of models based on its historic use. In a relatively short period of time since, Panerai has established itself as a brand for the rugged individual, based on the wartime acts of heroism which shaped it for its new civilian role.

IWC B-Uhr (1940)

Wristwatches proved their usefulness in coordinating the timing of mass attacks during World War One. As World War Two loomed, armed forces on all sides saw the value of reliable, standard-issue watches. Germany's newly reconstituted air force, the Luftwaffe, was no exception.

At the end of World War One, Germany was obliged by the Treaty of Versailles to destroy all its military aircraft, and was barred from having an air force. Germany complied but continued to train military pilots in secret. Sometimes this was under the pretence of preparing them for roles in civil aviation; but it also operated secret training camps at several military airfields in the Soviet Union.

One of Hitler's first acts after he came to power in 1933 was to create the *Reichsluftfahrtministerium* (RLM or Reich Aviation Ministry), which brought all the nation's flying organizations together under the banner of the *Deutscher Luftsportverband* (DLV or German Air Sports Association). Less than two months later it unveiled the military wing of the so-called Sports Association: the Luftwaffe – the Air Force. From its inception the Luftwaffe was preparing for war, with a specific interest in dive-bombing and long-range bombing missions, as a

paper on strategic theory, translated as *The Conduct of the Aerial War*, made clear in 1935.

Given such evidence of long-term planning, it is perhaps surprising that the need for a standard Luftwaffe watch was only addressed in 1940, a year after Hitler's invasion of Poland started World War Two. The result, after much consultation, was the B-Uhr. *Uhr* is the German for 'watch' (plural *Uhren*), and B stands for *Beobachtung*, meaning 'observation'.

Five different watch manufacturers won contracts to supply the B-Uhr. Stowa, Laco, Wempe and A. Lange & Söhne in Germany, and the International Watch Company (IWC) in Switzerland, had to comply with specifications laid down by the Reich Aviation Ministry in document Fl. 23883, a number engraved inside the back of every B-Uhr.

As long as they did so, there was a certain latitude in matters of design and function. Each of the five, for example, used a different movement. The B-Uhr was intended for navigation in battle conditions, in the confined space of a cockpit, and on night-time air raids. It was a large beast, fully 55mm in diameter, using movements borrowed from its manufacturers' pocket watch models. Its strap was extra-long, so that it could be worn outside an airman's uniform; and it had an enlarged crown so that it could be wound while wearing gloves.

A Baumuster, a version of IWC's B-Uhr, made for the German airforce, the Luftwaffe, in 1940.

Above: Luftwaffe Junkers Ju-52 bombers on a training mission in 1935, four years before the outbreak of World War Two.

Left: The B-Uhr had an extra large crown so that airmen could use it at chilly altitudes without removing their gloves.

All B-Uhren were anti-magnetic, an essential quality to prevent interference during use in the iron hull of an aeroplane.

B-Uhren manufactured before 1941 had a dial of classic simplicity: a central sweeping second hand, with Arabic hour indices set inside a single outer scale of sixty divisions, known as Baumuster ('type') A. From 1941 onwards the hour indices were replaced with minutes, at five-minute intervals; and the hours appeared within a smaller circle in the middle of the dial. The hour hand did not extend outside this inner circle; and this separation of hours and minutes made the watch much easier to consult for navigation purposes. The hands were luminous blue swords, and a luminous triangle at 12 o'clock helped orientate the dial, accompanied on the Baumuster A by two dots.

Unlike other military watches, for example the American A-11, the B-Uhr was not given to the airmen who used it: it was merely lent. Navigators had to sign their watches out before a mission and hand them back in when they returned. Once they were airborne, they received, by radio, a time signal from their airbase, synchronized with the German Naval Observatory – the official keeper of German standard time. B-Uhren could be hacked – that is, stopped by pulling out the crown, then restarted at the moment when the airbase's signal came through. In this way, every bomber on the same mission was working to the same time schedule.

Because they were checked back in after each mission, relatively few B-Uhren were made – one estimate suggests as few as 5,000 in total from all five companies involved – and correspondingly fewer originals have survived. Today they command very high prices among collectors.

There is some hope for those with smaller pockets: all five original manufacturers are still in business, even if under different ownership. Although the only *Beobachtungsuhren* made by Wempe and Lange & Söhne are those that survived the war, the other three makers have all produced modern watches derived from their 1940s models. Laco and Stowa both make contemporary versions of both the A and B dials, in a range of sizes from 40mm to 45mm – not quite as large as the original parent watch, but otherwise adhering to the simple, elegant spirit of clarity embodied by it.

IWC however, had developed a range of watches still intended for use by the original clientele – airmen. Now called the Big Pilot Watch, IWC's is the only descendant of the B-Uhr to retain its anti-magnetic feature. All the watches in the range now have a dial at 3 o'clock indicating how much time remains of its eight-day power reserve. Some models also have a full date-day-month calendar. Today, actor Ewan McGregor and Rolling Stone Keith Richards are among the admirers of the IWC B-Uhr.

There have been more than a hundred editions of the IWC Big Pilot Watch since it was launched in 2002, including some with a variation of the Baumuster B dial. In fact, IWC stopped producing the B-Uhr before the introduction of the Baumuster B and only ever made Baumuster A versions. It may be that the company's location in neutral Switzerland made trading with Germany difficult. IWC made 1,200 B-Uhren – but supplied only 1,000 to the Luftwaffe. With commendable Swiss balance, IWC sold the remaining 200 to Britain's Royal Air Force. Schaffhausen, where IWC still makes its watches, is on the north bank of the River Rhine, in a little bulge of Switzerland that sticks out into Germany. Whether by accident or design, the IWC factory was bombed in 1944 – not by Germany and German navigators wearing B-Uhren, but by the United States Army Air Force, wearing A-11s (see page 54).

American A-11 US military (1942)

An object lesson in simple, practical watch design, the A-11 was standard issue for thousands of American airmen and ground troops during World War Two. It's hard to believe that it was designed by a committee, and an army committee at that.

An old joke goes that a camel is a horse designed by a committee – one in which every member wants their own ideas to be adopted. The result is that all their bad ideas are included in the finished design, producing a misshapen beast instead of the magnificent thoroughbred horse that could have resulted from the hands of a single visionary artist.

The horse, of course, is by no means perfect; and the camel's strange feet and humps are well-adapted to its environment. It's the same with the A-11. It's no designer classic, but it was rigorously specified, well-engineered and got the job done. For Americans, at least, it is 'the watch that won the war'.

A-11 is the reference number of the military document that laid out the minimum specifications for the watch. It was published under the auspices of three high-level bodies – the US Army Air Forces, the Bureau of Aeronautics and the Air Council of the United Kingdom. The A-11 wasn't the only standard issue watch adopted by the Allies in World War Two, but it was one of the most widely distributed.

Watches had proved themselves in the military sphere three decades earlier, during World War One. Coordinated assaults on enemy lines required co-ordinated timing, and saw the birth of the command 'Synchronize your watches'. In that earlier conflict, with watches that lacked a second hand, that meant an accuracy of plus or minus 30 seconds; and one of the minimum requirements that the army set out in A-11 was the ability to 'hack' a watch.

This is not hacking in the modern, digital sense of the word, but a function which we all take for granted now with analogue watches. When you pull the crown out, the movement stops and you can adjust the time. The second hand also stops; and its circulation, along with that of the hour and minute hands, only starts again when the crown is pushed back in. Now, imagine a room full of troops who, on the command 'Synchronize your watches' all pull their crowns out when their second hands reach 12, and all then set their watches to an agreed time a minute or two in the future. When that time comes, on the command 'Hack!', they all restart their watches. Now every watch in the room is synchronized to the very second.

The A-11 was the first military watch to have a sweeping central second hand. The hour indices were complete – all 12 in Arabic numerals – in white

An off-white dial variation of a well-worn early US Army issue Elgin A-11 watch with characteristic brass case and canvas strap.

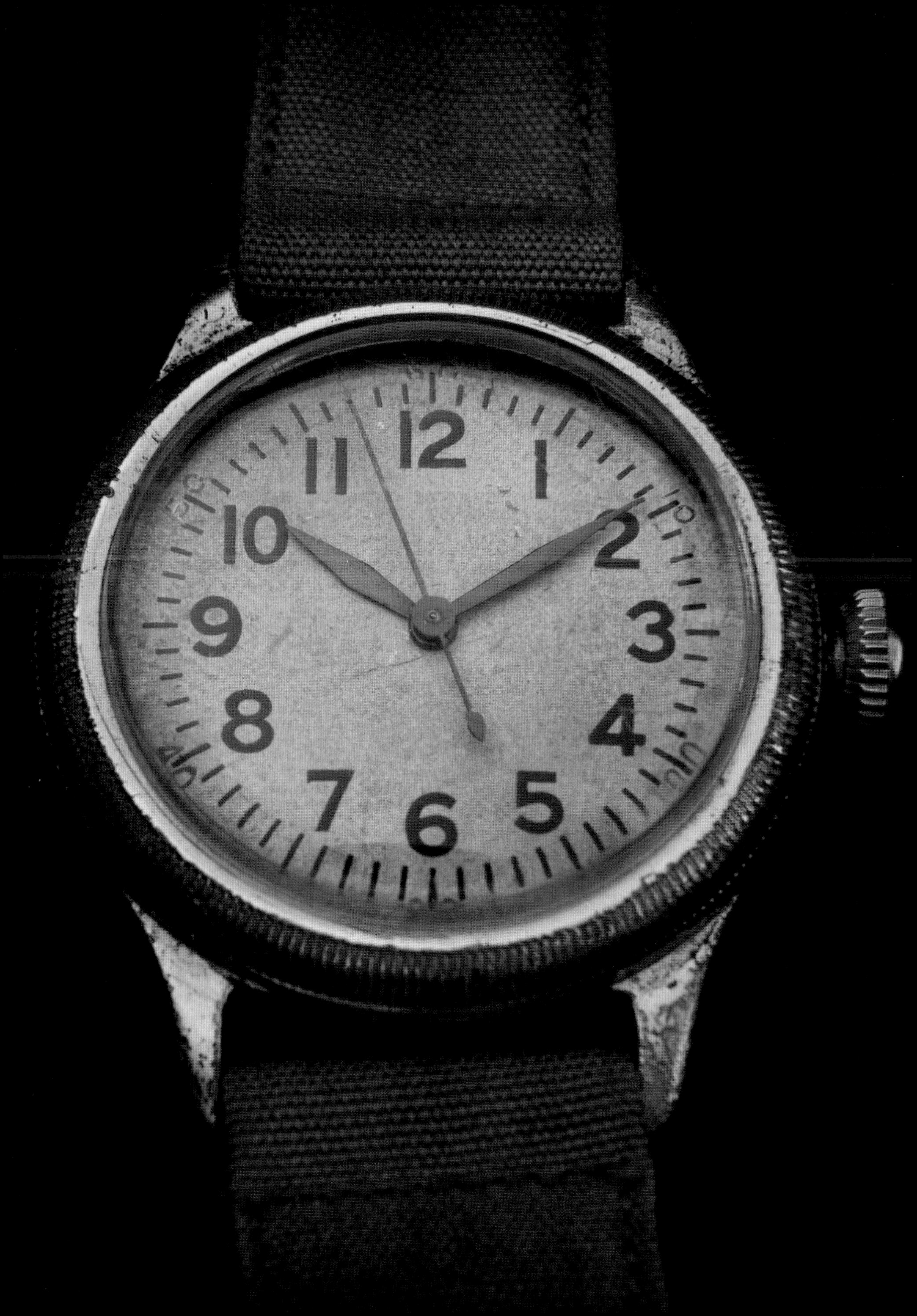
12
1
2
3
4
5
6
7
8
9
10
11

With the back plate removed, this A-11 reveals its manufacturer and country of origin, and confirms that it contains the regulation number of jewels.

American troops approach Omaha Beach in Normandy on D-Day – 6 June 1944, the largest seaborne invasion ever undertaken.

on a black dial, surrounded by an outer railroad-style minute scale. In addition, those A-11s issued to airmen all had luminous indices (although not always those of paratroopers and ground troops). This was a watch designed to be as readable as possible under wartime conditions, to minimize the possibility of human error.

There were other wartime considerations. Steel was a metal in high demand for ships and armaments of all kinds, and not to be used in manufacturing where other metals would do. The casing of the A-11 was to be made in brass. In practice it was chrome-plated, which helped to protect the softer brass from corrosion and wear. Brass too had a military role to play, and sometimes the A-11 cases were made of silver. The crystal must of course be unbreakable, and therefore acrylic.

Attention was also paid to the reliability of the movement. It was to be manually wound, and to have a minimum of fifteen jewels – jewels, which are harder than metals, are used in watches at points of movement most vulnerable to friction. In practice the need for a sweeping second hand was most easily solved by adding a sixteenth ruby.

Manufacture of the watch was entrusted to three American watchmakers – Elgin, Bulova and Waltham. They had to adhere to the strict specifications of the A-11 document, and there was little scope or need for variation. Nevertheless, there was some. There were small differences in the dials and hands; and each company used its own choice of movement. The Elgins were powered by the calibre 539, the Bulovas by the calibre 10AK CHS, and the Walthams by a 6.0 Premier movement. The A-11 was relatively small by today's standards, usually only 32mm in diameter (although this too

varied), and with a 16mm strap, either one- or two-piece, of olive canvas.

The watches were produced in their tens of thousands, and with such high levels of reliability, there are still plenty around today. Collectors are less likely, however, to find one with an original strap or in anything approaching original condition. The chrome-plated brass was simply not as hard-wearing as steel. Their backs always have a story to tell, inscribed with a multitude of numbers – serial, ordnance and part numbers, type of watch (A-11), manufacturer and which branch of the services (usually 'A.F. U.S. Army'). To complicate matters, the A-11 was also supplied, sometimes under different names, to the Canadian, British and Soviet air forces.

The watchmaking industry is keenly aware of the A-11's history, and of the marketability of its heritage. Anniversary recreations of classic designs in their original form are commonplace. The A-11, this most ordinary-looking, most widely worn wristwatch, has now been reproduced for the modern market – but, surprisingly, not by any of the three brands whose heritage it represents. Praesidus, a company formed only in the second decade of the current century, has brought out a meticulously accurate copy, most closely modelled on the Waltham version, which had the best readability of the three originals.

The Praesidus revival comes in its original 32mm dimensions and in a larger, 38mm version. Like the pilots' wartime models, it has fully luminous hour numbers and hands, which Praesidus offers either white or aged. And although it acknowledges that most wearers may prefer a leather strap, the new A-11 has an original olive canvas option. Eighty years on, it seems that some things cannot be improved upon.

'It's no designer classic, but it was rigorously specified, well-engineered and got the job done. For Americans, at least, it is "the watch that won the war".'

Omega Seamaster (1948)

Derived from a watch first designed for the British military, the Omega Seamaster became the watch that every diver wanted. Today, it is the oldest watch still being produced by the company.

The Omega Marine was the world's first watch designed for and commercially available to divers, outstripping the Rolex Oyster, which declared itself in 1926 to be merely the world's first *waterproof* watch. Launched in 1932, the Marine enclosed the whole watch inside a second, outer casing, and sealed the edges with cork. The system, originally conceived by Louis Alix in Geneva, was inspired in its simplicity: the deeper the diver, the greater the pressure on the outer casing and the tighter the seal. The Marine was successfully tested, first at the bottom of Lake Geneva, some 75m (246ft) deep, and subsequently by the Swiss Laboratory of Horology at a simulated depth of 135m (443ft). Among its wearers was William Beebe, a deep-sea explorer and early ecologist who wore it during dives in Otis Barton's bathysphere in the 1930s. Beebe became the first naturalist to observe marine life in its natural habitat, diving in the pressurized vehicle to depths of up to 923m (3,028ft).

Another Marine fan was Yves Le Prieur, a French naval officer and pilot. Le Prieur was a compulsive inventor – he undertook the first flight on Japanese soil when, while serving as a military attaché in Tokyo, he collaborated with two Japanese enthusiasts on the construction of a glider. During World War One he invented an air-to-air missile system, the Le Prieur rocket launcher, for shooting down German observation balloons. After the war, Le Prieur developed the scuba tank and facemask which helped to popularize diving as a leisure activity. Today he is regarded as the father of modern diving, and certainly his experience contributed to the development of the Seamaster.

When Omega wanted to launch a new everyday men's watch, they decided to incorporate Louis Alix's waterproofing seal, replacing the cork with a rubber O-ring. The Seamaster was aimed not at divers but at gentlemen, advertised at its launch in 1948 as a watch for 'town, sea, and country'. Nevertheless, it was waterproof to a depth of 60m (197ft), which was demonstrated when a diver, Gordon McLean, took it to 62.5m (205ft) off the coast of Australia in 1955. As further proof of its hardiness the Seamaster was fixed the following year to the outside of a Douglas DC-6 aircraft and flown over the North Atlantic – some say, over the North Pole.

In 1957, Omega built on the Seamaster name with three new watches for more professional users of the chronometer. The Railmaster, aimed not at train spotters but at scientists, boasted a high resistance to magnetic interference. The Speedmaster (see page 86) was for motor racing enthusiasts, timing the

Two versions of the Seamaster, the oldest design still in production at Omega – above, the original from 1948; and below, a 300 model for divers from 1957.

Actor Pierce Brosnan in his debut as James Bond, the film *GoldenEye* (1995), wearing an Omega Seamaster 300M Ref. 2541.80.

Aquanaut Jacques Cousteau (1910–97), the first recipient of the Seamaster 1000.

performance of cars to the split second. The third was the Seamaster 300, designed with a simplified face and more emphatic hands – the hour hand was now an arrow and not merely a pointer.

The Seamaster 300 built on the success among divers of the original Seamaster. The name was a direct challenge to another much-admired diving watch of the time, the Blancpain Fifty Fathoms (see page 70); 50 fathoms were still only 91.5m (300ft). It announced Omega's belief that the watch could now withstand the pressure at depths of up to 300m (984ft), although in truth the testing equipment of the day could only simulate 200m (656ft). The Seamaster 300 received the ultimate endorsement for a diver's watch when it was worn by Frenchman Jacques Cousteau. Cousteau invented the aqualung and brought diving into the living room with a string of popular TV series that simultaneously celebrated sea life and the sport of scuba diving, using his ship the *Calypso* as a base for underwater exploration.

Competition among diver's watch manufacturers intensified during the 1960s and 1970s. Rolex produced its Sea Dweller model in 1967, waterproof to a depth of more than 600m (1,969ft) and Omega struck back with the Seamaster 600, known popularly as the PloProf – an abbreviation of the French *plongeur professionel*, meaning 'professional diver'. The Seamaster 1000, released in 1971, was nicknamed the Grand because it was waterproof at 1,000m (3,281ft). It was created as the result of a commission by Prince Rainier III of Monaco for 50 timepieces to reward supporters of the Monaco Oceanographic Research Institute and Museum, and tested by attaching it to the outside of the submarine *Beaver IV* which dived to more than 1,000m. The first recipient was Jacques Cousteau. It remains the most waterproof watch that Omega has ever produced, and it has never failed. However, it was rather bulky and not as popular as earlier variations; even after it was made available to the public, fewer than 100 more were produced, making it one of the most collectable in the range. An updated version in 1976 found only around 300 buyers. Up to 100 more were made during the prototype stage. The Grand was discontinued in 1982. Several attempts at an electronic version foundered because low temperature at depth quickly drained the battery. The Seamaster PloProf was revived in 2009, now with a claimed resistance of 1,200m (3,937ft) and remains in production today.

The Seamaster took a definite step into the mainstream consciousness in 1995 in its latest guise as the Seamaster Diver 300M, when Pierce Brosnan made his debut in the role of British spy James Bond. In the original novels, Ian Fleming specified the Rolex Submariner (see page 74) as Bond's watch of choice; and the Submariner appears on Sean Connery, George Lazenby and Roger Moore. Connery also wore a Gruen from time to time, and the Geiger counter watch in *Thunderball* was a Breitling Top Time. Moore was the first Bond whose watches were imbued with other functions – a circular saw, for example, or a bullet-deflecting magnet. In his long tenure in the role he wore a variety of Seiko analogue and digital watches, and his successor Timothy Dalton used first a Seiko then, returning to Bond's roots, a Submariner.

After Dalton's very short stint as Bond, the franchise reinvented itself with bigger, bolder stunts than ever before, and a wave of income-generating product placement. The vodka in the agent's trademark martini – shaken, not stirred – gave way to gin, and there was even an official Bond beer, Heineken. And for the first time, in Brosnan's debut, Bond wore an Omega Seamaster. He has done so ever since, whether played by Brosnan or Daniel Craig. The Brosnan Bond's choice of wristwatch introduced the Seamaster to a new world of celebrity, a place where non-divers wanted its status. Most poignant among its new admirers, Princess Diana made a gift of one to her son Prince William only a few days before her death in 1997.

By the time Craig took over, a host of new variations had joined the Seamaster family. The Seamaster Planet Ocean was a luxury diving watch to be worn in and out of the sea. The Seamaster Aqua Terra, however, was a return to the styling of the very first Seamaster, waterproof but without the rotating bezel seen on all models from 1957 onwards. Then in 2007, on the 50th anniversary of that first expansion of the range, Omega released faithful reproductions of the Railmaster, the Speedmaster and the Seamaster 300. It followed this nostalgia-inducing trilogy with, in 2018, a 70th anniversary recreation of the 1948 Seamaster.

With the Seamaster 300 and its successors, Omega has successfully fought a running battle with Rolex for the crown of the world's most waterproof watch. Rolex set a new record in 2012 when *Titanic* director James Cameron wore a Rolex Deep Sea during a dive in the Challenger Deep to 10,907m (35,784ft). Omega countered in 2018 with a prototype, the Seamaster Planet Ocean Ultra Deep Professional, which withstood the water 10,928m (35,853ft) below the surface in the Mariana Trench, the deepest water in the world.

Jaeger-LeCoultre Memovox (1950)

The aftermath of World War Two saw the emergence of a new world order – a world of increasing prosperity and consumerism, in which communism was the enemy and capitalism was king. Watches were designed for busy businessmen, and in America the frenzy of anti-communist sentiment knew no bounds.

Communism was anti-American, and therefore (according to US Senator Joe McCarthy's wrong-headed logic) anything anti-American was communist. He pursued a terrifying personal and public vendetta against anyone he perceived as being critical of the USA's unfettered approach to capitalism. Artists of all kinds were a particular focus of his paranoia, and none more so than those working in Hollywood, California – the movie capital of the world. Hundreds of actors, directors, scriptwriters and behind-the-scenes staff were black-listed for imaginary threats to the American way of life. Some were only able to work under assumed names while others fled the country.

These were not only 'little people' with no power to defend themselves: they included high profile leading names of American and world cinema. One of them, the silent movie star Charlie

Chaplin, was a legend of the industry. Not only one of its most famous performers, Chaplin had also formed the production company United Artists, along with fellow actors Mary Pickford and Douglas Fairbanks and pioneering director D.W. Griffiths, to give cinema artists more control over their finances and artistic output.

Perhaps this enterprise of mutual support is what drew McCarthy's ire. The senator mobilized a damaging campaign of smears and character attacks on Chaplin that ruined his reputation and box office appeal. One of McCarthy's closest colleagues, John E. Rankin, brought the matter to Congress, where he declared that '[Chaplin's] very life in Hollywood is detrimental to the moral fabric of America'. He called for Chaplin to be expelled not only from Hollywood but from the country, in which case 'his loathsome pictures can be kept from before the eyes of the American youth. He should be deported and gotten rid of at once'.

When Charlie Chaplin sailed from America to England in 1952 to attend a premiere in London, his visa to re-enter the US was revoked. He would not return to America for 20 years, and instead bought a villa near Lake Geneva, in the Swiss canton of Vaud. He had fallen in love with the country during a visit in 1931; and now, Switzerland

The Jaeger-LeCoultre Memovox presented to Charlie Chaplin in 1953 to celebrate his decision to live in Switzerland.

Charlie Chaplin (1889–1977) in his film *Limelight*, which he was promoting in London when his visa to return to the US was revoked.

In 1953, President Harry S. Truman (left) was presented with the Memovox's rival, a Cricket wristwatch, which was the first to include an alarm clock function.

was delighted to have him back. America might have chased Chaplin away, but Vaud welcomed him with open arms, and a generous gift: a Jaeger-LeCoultre Memovox wristwatch.

Often cited as the world's first wristwatch with a built-in alarm, the Memovox debuted in 1950. In fact, it had a predecessor in the Cricket, an alarm wristwatch launched in 1947 by a small Swiss company called Vulcain. The Cricket achieved considerable success when US President Harry S. Truman was photographed wearing one. Vulcain made the most of this high-ranking boost and presented several subsequent White House occupants with the model.

The Cricket was, however, an imperfect response to the challenge of incorporating an alarm clock in a watch. The use of two barrels was innovative and meant that the alarm did not drain the power reserve of the main movement; but it also resulted in only being able to adjust the hour and minute hands forwards. The Cricket used a fourth hand to set the alarm time, adjusted by a button separate from the crown, reaching beyond the hour hand to an outer index divided into tens of minutes, numbered at 10, 30 and 50. The use of a membrane to sound the alarm, and a perforated double back to amplify its volume, made for a loud ring, not unlike that of the insect from which the watch took its name; but the watch produced a constant and less welcome drone, which on more than one occasion was mistaken for a bomb in the White House.

The Memovox was an advance on the Cricket. Here was a watch aimed squarely at the Busy Man, the executive with a string of meetings to attend every day. 'Memovox reminds – warns – awakens' was the advertising slogan for the new model.

It had two power reserves, with a crown for each. Its alarm was set not with a hand but by a large rotatable central disc fully half the diameter of the main dial, with a pointer which could be set to a separate hour scale printed outside it on the main dial. Above all, Jaeger-LeCoultre was able to bring a sense of flair and elegance to the Memovox. The strap lugs were hooded; the crowns were of different sizes, to distinguish them; and, of course, it bore the exquisite lettering of the Jaeger-LeCoultre signature.

The Cricket's layout placed two identical scales – the alarm time and the hour-minute index – right next to each other; and its four hands and two sets of numerals – hour and alarm minutes – made for a cluttered dial. The Memovox, in contrast, bore only a full set of simple sans serif hour numerals in gold. The hour-minute and alarm scales were distinct from each other and the whole appearance was one of perfect clarity.

The Memovox presented to Charlie Chaplin was engraved on the back: *Hommage du gouvernement Vaudois à Charlie Chaplin – 6 Octobre 1953* – 'homage from the Vaud government to Charlie Chaplin'. It was the almost perfect gift, with one notable mistake. Chaplin was left-handed and preferred to wear a watch on his right wrist, with the crown on the left of the watch. The great comedian owned a left-handed Rolex Oyster with this arrangement, as well as a (right-handed) gold IWC automatic watch and another Jaeger-LeCoultre piece, an Atmos clock with which he was presented in 1972 by Swiss press photographers for his ever-welcoming attitude to the nation's journalists.

The Atmos is lost now; but Jaeger-LeCoultre found an identical example and presented it to the Chaplin World museum which now occupies his villa in Vaud. Elsewhere in the building there also resides, in a secure glass case, the actual Memovox with which Chaplin was welcomed to his new home back in 1953.

Patek Philippe 2499 (1950)

Patek Philippe's revision of its classic model 1518 was no less desirable than its predecessor. So few were made that each one has a story to tell – but none more so than the one owned, all too briefly, by John Lennon. It's a story of love, death, betrayal, theft and – at last – recovery.

Only 349 Patek Philippe 2499s were made during its 35 years of production. Their scarcity alone makes them among the most collectable of watches. They were bigger than the 1518 and managed to retain the values of the original with an appearance more in keeping with modern fashion. Their price tag meant that only the rich and famous could afford them – and any connection with celebrity only adds to the auction price for any that come up for sale today.

It was just such a potential sale that brought the story of one such watch out into the open. A collector brought his 2499 to Christie's auction house in Geneva, with a view to selling it. In light of the watch's original owner, Christie's approached the owner's widow for confirmation of its provenance – and the whole sensational history of the watch unfolded, with the help of the police and the courts.

The watch once belonged to John Lennon. His wife Yoko Ono gave it to him as a present on his 40th birthday in October 1980. She bought it at Tiffany & Co, and the dial bears not only the name of Patek Philippe, but also that of the store from which it was bought. Already there are numerous factors to inflate the potential interest of bidders – the dial, the shop, the buyer, the recipient and the occasion. Add to them the fact that Lennon was shot dead only six weeks after he was given the watch, and it is an artefact steeped in love and tragedy.

More was to come, however. When Christie's asked Ono about it, she thought that it must be a fake because, as far as she knew, the real watch was safely locked up in storage along with other of Lennon's items from which she could not bear to be parted. But it wasn't there; and details confirmed by Ono proved that Christie's really did have John Lennon's watch. How had the seller – an Italian dealer living in Asia, who insisted that he had bought it in good faith – come by it? Working backwards, the Swiss and German police were able to piece together the watch's journey.

The Italian had bought the watch in a private sale from Berlin house Auctionata in 2014. He paid €600,000 for it and knew of its existence because he was on Auctionata's board of advisors. Was this an abuse of his position for personal gain? And how had Auctionata acquired the 2499?

A Patek Philippe 2499 from 1971, one of only 349 produced between 1951 and 1986 – this one, from the Third Series production, has the days and months in French, and the name of the retailer.

John Lennon (1940–80) photographed at The Hit Factory, NYC in 1980, wearing his 40th birthday present from Yoko Ono, a Patek Philippe 2499 Fourth Series.

A Patek Philippe 2499 Fourth Series version, identical to John Lennon's, marked with the same retailer's name as Lennon's, Tiffany & Co.

Despite the hefty injection of cash from the Italian, Auctionata filed for bankruptcy in 2017. In the process of disposing of its remaining assets, another 86 items which once belonged to John Lennon were discovered. They had been sold to Auctionata by a German man, who declared in an accompanying letter that he could not prove his ownership or disprove Yoko Ono's. The man, known in subsequent police reports only as Erhan, insisted that he had been given them – no doubt also 'in good faith' – in Turkey, by a Turkish man called Koral Karsan.

From Switzerland to Germany to Turkey, now the trail led right back to the Dakota Building in New York in which Lennon and Ono were living at the time of Lennon's assassination on the pavement outside it. Koral Karsan was the former chauffeur of Yoko Ono, and a man with a grudge. In 2006, he claimed to have had a sexual relationship with Ono, and tried to blackmail her to the tune of $2 million over the existence of compromising photos and audio tapes which he'd secretly been recording. He threatened to murder Yoko Ono and her son if she did not pay; but Ono went to the police instead, and Karsan was deported to his native Turkey. He was one of the few people who had access to the storage where Ono believed the watch was locked; and he had been stealing John Lennon's belongings all along.

While all this was being uncovered by police investigations, the watch itself was held in Geneva and classified as stolen property. There then followed a lengthy court case between Yoko Ono and the Italian dealer over the current ownership of the watch. Ono knew that she had owned it because it was itemized among those possessions of Lennon's which she had inherited after his death. The chain of misdemeanours connecting Karsan, Erhan, Auctionata and the Italian rather undermined the claim of the latter, and the court in Geneva found in favour of Ono. At time of writing, an appeal is underway.

The very public twists and turns of the tale of John Lennon's watch must make it one of the most famous watches in the world, and therefore one of the most valuable. The only other Tiffany-stamped 2499 known to exist was sold by Sotheby's in 2020 for $818,600 by an owner with none of the celebrity of Lennon or the back story of the Beatle's watch.

A different pair of 2499s make an interesting comparison. In 1987, Patek Philippe made two platinum versions of the 2499. One went straight into the Patek Philippe museum in Geneva; the other eventually found its way into the collection of rock guitarist and watch connoisseur Eric Clapton, a man whose contribution to popular music could be said to rival Lennon's. When Clapton sold it through Christie's in 2012, it fetched $3.6 million.

Ringo Starr, another Beatle, sold his Patek Philippe 3448 at auction in 2015 for a mere $180,000. But the 3448 is not the 2499, and Starr is not Lennon. Estimates for the value of Lennon's watch vary widely, from $3 million to $40 million, depending on what one dealer called 'the right messaging and marketing'. It's all hypothetical. Yoko Ono is now in her nineties, and assuming that she retains ownership of her gift to John, she is unlikely to want to sell it now. Their son Sean Lennon then stands to inherit not only the weight of the legacy of two such celebrated parents but a wristwatch with a provenance like no other.

One mystery surrounding the watch remains. One of the identifying features of the watch, which enabled Yoko Ono to confirm its identity, was the inscription on the back. Before she gave it to John, she had Tiffany engrave it with a single word. That word remains a closely guarded secret, and the court transcripts reveal only that: '[Ono] had the inscription ___ engraved on the back in reference to the first song ___ from the album ___ that the couple had composed together after a period of separation.' The clues are there, but the answer is not.

Blancpain Fifty Fathoms (1953)

'Blancpain has never made a quartz watch and never will.' This is one of the slogans of the oldest watch brand in the world. It's been a close-run thing at times, and the company owes much of its survival to its legendary diving watch, the Fifty Fathoms.

Blancpain was founded in 1735 in Villeret (pronounced Ville-Ray), in northwestern Switzerland, by the town's mayor, Jehan-Jacques Blancpain. The company remained in the control of the Blancpain family for the next 197 years. Among its many milestones was the production of the world's first self-winding wristwatch, using a mechanism invented by English watchmaker, John Hardwood, in 1926.

Following the death of Frédéric-Emile Blancpain in 1931, however, his daughter and heir Berthe-Nellie showed no interest in taking the reins. Instead, the following year, two of Frédéric-Emile's closest colleagues bought the company. Under Swiss law at the time, the new owners André Léal and Betty Fiechter were barred from retaining the business name. Instead they called the company Rayville, a phonetic reversal of its home town; but there was nothing to stop them using the name Blancpain on its products or perpetuating the quality on which its founding fathers had built their reputation.

Betty Fiechter was still involved in 1953, when Rayville-Blancpain launched the watch for which it is best known, the Fifty Fathoms diving watch. The success of the Fifty Fathoms caught Fiechter by surprise: by the end of the decade, the company was producing 100,000 watches a year and still struggling to keep up with demand. It joined the consortium La Société Suisse pour l'Industrie Horlogère (SSIH), which included Tissot, Lemania and Omega, to take advantage of its greater production resources.

The SSIH was hit hard by the Quartz Crisis of the 1970s and 1980s, and it was not alone. The other large consortium of Swiss watchmakers, Das Allgemeine Gesellschaft der Schweizerischen Uhrenindustrie AG (ASUAG), was also in trouble. In alarm, the two bodies' Swiss bankers called time on their independent but overlapping activities and in 1983 demanded a merger. The new organization was La Société de Microélectronique et d'Horlogerie (SMH), now known as the Swatch Group, of which Blancpain remains a part.

Without the Fifty Fathoms, it is possible that the name Blancpain would have disappeared altogether. It arrived at a fortuitous time, however, riding – as it were – on the crest of a wave of waterproof watches and just ahead of that other great modern diving watch, the Rolex Submariner (see page 74). World War Two had

An original edition Blancpain Fifty Fathoms diver's watch from 1953.

Jean-Jacques Fiechter, CEO of Blancpain from 1950 to 1980, whose diving experiences in the south of France helped the development of the Fifty Fathoms watch.

A 50th anniversary edition of the Fifty Fathoms, released in 2003, remains true to the distinctive character of the original.

driven new technology in water resistance, in the service of covert marine operations. In its wake, diving increased in popularity as a leisure activity.

The man driving developments at Rayville-Blancpain was Jean-Jacques Fiechter, nephew of Betty, whom she brought in as CEO in 1950. Jean-Jacques was an enthusiastic amateur diver, who had come up against the need for a reliable underwater watch when – not wearing one – he ran out of air in his aqualung in the waters of the Mediterranean off the south of France.

The resulting timepiece was the culmination of four years of research into what a diver needs and how Blancpain could supply it. It was named the Fifty Fathoms after the depth to which it was guaranteed – a fathom is a nautical measurement of depth, equivalent to 1.83m (6ft), and the new watch was reckoned to be good to 100m (328ft), the furthest a diver could reach with the oxygen tanks of the day.

It solved many of the problems inherent in designing a diver's watch. It had a double-sealed crown to guard against accidental pulling during a dive; and an automatic movement, which reduced the amount of wear on that double seal by removing the need to wind the watch. The screw-on caseback was sealed with a rubber O-ring, and the O-ring was anchored in a channel with an intermediate metal ring to stop it from twisting out of shape when the back was screwed on and off. The Fifty Fathoms was given an iron inner case to protect it against irregular magnetic influence; and a rotating bezel which a diver could set to know exactly how much oxygen they had used and how much they had left.

The bezel was luminous, and made of Bakelite, the first plastic to be made entirely from synthetic materials. Bakelite had transformed the design world since its development in 1909 by Belgian industrialist Leo Baekeland. This was one of the first times it was used in watchmaking and gave the Fifty Fathoms a unique appearance. To prevent a diver accidentally moving the bezel during a dive – and losing track of their remaining air – Fiechter devised a patent locking mechanism, which meant the bezel could only be turned with the downward pressure of three fingers on it.

Soon after the Fifty Fathoms' debut, Fiechter was lucky enough to be approached by Commando Hubert, the new elite combat swimmers unit of the French special forces. It had been disappointed by the results of tests of other diving watches and acquired a Fifty Fathoms for further trials. The dial of Fiechter's watch was larger and more visible than those which Commando Hubert had been trying out, and its 38-hour power reserve outperformed that of its rivals. Above all, it was fully waterproof at depth. Combat swimmer Lieutenant Claude Riffaud wrote enthusiastically to Blancpain's distributor: 'The water resistance that we have tested to 100 metres is perfect, the operation is excellent and the luminosity matches requirements. During a dive, one of these watches was lost at a depth of 53 metres. We found it 24 hours later in perfect condition and still running smoothly.'

Fifty Fathoms watches were soon being supplied to several of the world's navies. A final defining feature of the Fifty Fathoms was added to satisfy the requirements of one particularly large potential market, the US Navy. The Fifty Fathoms met that navy's specifications in all but one respect – the US Navy insisted on a moisture indicator, to be visible within the dial without impeding the movement of the hands. Fiechter's solution was ingenious: he added a small circle, of which one half was pale blue and the other red. If for any reason the watch's water resistance was damaged and water had found its way in, in any small measure, the blue half of the circle would turn red. Therefore, at the start of their mission, a US diver could know instantly whether that most vital of tools, the diver's watch, was still up to the job.

Rolex Submariner (1953)

If imitation is the sincerest form of flattery, then the Rolex Submariner must be the most admired watch in the world. It is certainly the model for the greatest number of counterfeits. There's no substitute for the real thing, however, as Sean Connery would have told you.

Competition is fierce for the title of first diver's watch to be workable at a depth of 100m (328ft). Blancpain's Fifty Fathoms (see page 70) was launched a year ahead of Rolex's Submariner, but the Submariner had been in production for a year before its launch. It's not important. What matters more than anything in the world of watches is status, and the Submariner has it in bucketfuls.

Before the Submariner, Rolex already had form in the sphere of waterproof watches. The Rolex Oyster, introduced in 1926, had a revolutionary case and a perpetual movement. With its reliability and style it played a central role in establishing the wristwatch as an item that people could wear all the time, not only on occasions when its water resistance was required.

Just as the Blancpain Fifty Fathoms was driven by its CEO Jean-Jacques Fiechter's enthusiasm for underwater sport, so too was the Submariner by Rolex's public relations director René-Paul Jeanneret.

Jeanneret, a keen leisure diver, had a friend in Jacques Cousteau, the pioneering undersea explorer whose films helped to popularize the activity. Cousteau, a former French naval officer, invented the aqualung, which delivered air from tanks to a diver only on demand and therefore greatly increased the length of time a diver could spend below the surface. Before Cousteau, tanks were simply 'on' all the time, continuously and wastefully issuing oxygen whether the diver needed it or not. Together, Cousteau and Jeanneret fine-tuned the Submariner to perfection.

Well, almost. The bezel of Blancpain's Fifty Fathoms was unidirectional and could only be turned in an anticlockwise direction. This was a safety feature, so that if it was accidentally moved during a dive, it meant the diver would only think they had less time remaining before they had to surface. Blancpain held the patent for this feature, and Rolex was unable to incorporate it in its watches until the 1980s.

Otherwise, the rivals were very similar in appearance and function; and in one crucial area Rolex was superior. The crown, with an axle leading directly from outside the watch to the heart of the movement, is the most vulnerable point of any water-resistant watch. Rolex had already dealt with this weakness in the Oyster, and now it introduced a double set of O-rings within the stem system so that

The Rolex Submariner, launched in 1953, one of the most counterfeited watches in the world.

All eyes were probably not on James Bond's Submariner 6538 in this scene from the character's first outing, *Dr No* (1962), starring Ursula Andress and Sean Connery.

Auguste Piccard's Trieste Bathyscaphe, which travelled to a depth of 3,131.8m (10,275ft) with a prototype Rolex Submariner strapped to the outside.

in or out, the crown was perfectly sealed and waterproof to 100m (328ft).

The Submariner was rigorously tested at France's Deep Sea Research Centre near Cannes, where 132 diving trials resulted in no failures at all. Even when the watch was lowered below its claimed limit, on a line to a depth of 120m (394ft), it was pulled up to the surface unscathed. In a separate test, an admittedly unique, specially constructed Rolex was strapped to the outside of Swiss submarine explorer Auguste Piccard's Bathyscaphe which then dived to a depth of 3,131.8m (10,275ft), returning with the watch in full working order.

The Submariner was a popular watch from the start, and Rolex continued to develop it with small improvements to its functions over the following 10 years. Each new version was given its own Rolex reference number to distinguish it from the launch model, the No. 6204. The No. 6200, which made its debut in 1955, had a thicker case and a larger, 8mm crown, and was succeeded in 1956 by the No. 6538, a similar watch with an upgraded movement. The No. 6536/1 of 1957 was the first to include a chronometer, but the function was soon added to the No. 6538, as the No. 6538/1.

While other brands have introduced wholesale changes to their classics over the years, trading as much on the name of the original watch as on the watch itself, Rolex has a reputation for resisting change when it comes to the redesign of its models over the years. Even today the complications and layout of the Submariner are recognizably those of the earliest versions, with modest cosmetic variations. Only in 1959 did the Submariner expand from its original 39mm diameter to a barely larger 40mm; and more than 60 years passed before its next imperceptible increase, to 41mm, in 2020. Why, the watch's many admirers argue, change a successful formula?

Admiration comes not only from the diving community. One wearer in particular was terrified by the diving he had to do, although his many achievements included battles with sharks in confined underwater spaces. Sean Connery, the actor who came to global fame in on-screen role of James Bond, wore a Submariner 6538 in the first three Bond films – *Dr No*, *From Russia with Love* and *Goldfinger*. The watch was, according to differing accounts, either his own property, or that of Cubby Broccoli, the producer of the films.

The association between watch and all-action hero has remained ever since. Other brands have sought to capitalize on the connection. Under Pierce Brosnan's and Daniel Craig's tenures of the role the watch of sponsored choice was an Omega Seamaster. But Roger Moore wore a Submariner 5513 in his first two outings as Bond – *Live and Let Die* and *The Man with the Golden Gun* – before transferring his allegiance to Seiko; and Timothy Dalton wore two versions of the Submariner in *Licence to Kill* – a 5513 and a 16610. George Lazenby also wore a 5513 in *On Her Majesty's Secret Service*, his sole performance as the spy – he had bought the watch himself for good luck, ahead of his audition for the part.

'Sean Connery, the actor who came to global fame in on-screen role of James Bond, wore a Submariner 6538 in the first three Bond movies ... The association between watch and all-action hero has remained ever since.'

Breitling Navitimer (1954)

The classic aviator's chronometer has become the wristwatch of choice for highflyers in all walks of life, from jazz musicians to racing drivers. Throughout its 70-year history it has maintained its original character, while the variations in its design over the decades have made it highly collectable.

Léon Breitling, born in a French-speaking canton of Switzerland, was fascinated by timepieces from an early age, and after serving an apprenticeship he set up his own company in 1884 at the age of 24. He became a master watchmaker, with a reputation for extreme precision, and eventually employed more than 50 people in his workshop in La Chaux-de-Fonds. After his death in 1914, the business maintained its reputation under his son Gaston, and after Gaston died in 1935, under his grandson Willy.

The Navitimer's history goes back to 1941, when Willy Breitling introduced the Chronomat model. The Breitling Chronomat was the first watch to incorporate a two-button stopwatch, and the first watch to include a circular slide rule in its movable outer bezel. It remains in production today; American comedian Jerry Seinfeld is among its devotees, and comedians know a thing or two about timing. The latest model was introduced in 2009.

In the early 1950s the Breitling company was approached by an American organization, the Aircraft Owners & Pilots Association (AOPA), who wanted to develop a wristwatch for its members. By then, Breitling already had a reputation in the aviation industry, having produced a precision chronograph for use in the cockpit which was eventually adopted by more than 30 airlines and, among others, Britain's Royal Air Force. The result, after close collaboration with the AOPA, was the Navitimer, launched in 1954. Initially available only to AOPA members, it was opened up for sale to the general public in 1956. Until then the watch bore only the AOPA's logo and not Breitling's winged B or the model number, in this case No. 806. That's one easy way to know whether an early Navitimer was one sold only to AOPA members or one bought on the open market.

The Navitimer was relatively large at 41mm in diameter, an advantage to pilots who needed to be able to see its display quickly and easily. Furthermore, it incorporated the Chronomat's slide rule, an indispensable aid to aviators who were making complex calculations about speed, time and fuel on the move. The three sub-dials were, like the rest of the watch, in stylish black. Not until the 1960s did they appear in a more readably contrasting white, a further distinction between earlier and later versions.

A Breitling Navitimer, c. 1950s. The Navitimer was conceived as an aid to the complex calculations required in airborne navigation.

Astronaut Scott Carpenter secured in position inside his Mercury-Atlas 7 capsule on 24 May 1962 with, among other things, a Breitling Navitimer strapped around his spacesuited wrist.

Actor John Travolta, a qualified pilot of Boeing 707, 737 and 747 airliners, endorses the Navitimer in an advertisement from 2006.

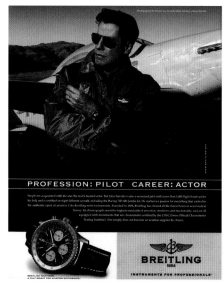

The AOPA watches were driven by the reliable Valjoux 72 mechanical movement. Valjoux is a relative youngster in the Swiss watch industry, established in 1901 by two brothers, John and Charles Reymond. After 18 months, Breitling switched to the Venus company, a business founded in 1923, and began to run Navitimers with the Venus 178, still regarded as one of the finest movements ever made. Venus movements are recognizable by the stamp of a small five-pointed star. During the crisis of confidence in Swiss watches prompted by the arrival of quartz movements from Japan, Venus struggled to survive, and in 1966 it was bought up by its old rival Valjoux. Today Valjoux movements appear in almost every global watch brand.

Willy Breitling began to steer the company to the high end of the market in the 1950s. When the Quartz Revolution began to unfold, his first move was to emphasize the brand's affinity with aviation. The Breitling B logo was framed from 1965 onwards not with two feathered wings but with two jets. The Navitimer was by then unquestionably the first choice for pilots around the world – and beyond. Scott Carpenter was a US Navy pilot and one of the original Project Mercury astronauts who launched America's space program in 1959. He pointed out to Breitling that a 12-hour watch was inadequate in the infinite darkness of space. If an astronaut lost track of time, how could they tell if it was 6.30 a.m. or 6.30 p.m? In response, Breitling produced the Cosmonaute Navitimer, a watch with a 24-hour dial, which Carpenter wore on his spacesuit as he piloted Mercury-Atlas 7 into orbit around the Earth. The watch's popularity was not confined to aeronauts. Other adventurers, those accustomed to pursuing extremes, also sported the Navitimer. Three Formula One champions of the 1960s wore one – Englishman Graham Hill, Scotsman Jim Clark and (fittingly) the Swiss driver Jo Siffert. Pushing the boundaries in a different way, jazz trumpet legend Miles Davis, another man for whom timing was key, wore a Navitimer in the 1960s and 1970s.

More design changes were to come. Size may not be everything; but just in case, Breitling launched its 'Big Case' Navitimers in 1968 – at 48mm in diameter, considerably larger than anything else on the market. To overcome the problems of a large watch balanced on a narrow wrist, it featured very short strap lugs; and its outsize novelty introduced the Navitimer to a new, younger, audience. The Big Case watches were, like all Navitimers to this point, hand-winders. The first commercially produced automatic watches – ones that didn't need to be wound by hand and which, more importantly, couldn't be overwound – were invented in the 1920s by English horologist, John Hardwood. Hardwood refined his 270° oscillating movement in Grenchen, Switzerland, where he found the necessary watchmaking expertise. Rolex cornered the market when it launched its own automatic movement, based on Hardwood's technology, but using a 360° rotor movement, in 1931, with the debut of the Oyster Perpetual. As quartz watches threatened to render obsolete the complex movements of the mechanical watch, several of the Swiss industry's big names were racing to produce a new automatic watch. Breitling continued to modernize in 1969 by introducing the first self-winding Navitimers, using a modular movement developed with Heuer, Hamilton and Buren. It did so just a few days ahead of the launch of Zenith's El Primero, which used a full-rotor process. The new Navitimer satisfied the quartz generation, which no longer expected to have to wind a watch regularly.

Navitimers were finally given a date window in the 1970s – a change too far for many of the watch's afficionados, who consider that addition to mark the end of the model's golden era. In the same decade, some versions even carried quartz movements and, more radically still, LED and LCD displays. Willy Breitling was still at the helm, but the struggle to compete in a technologically transformed world was proving to be a losing battle both for the company and for Willy's health. The next generation of the Breitling family showed little interest in the company, so Willy found a buyer for the brand and closed the Breitling factory in 1978. Willy himself died the following year.

The company passed to Ernst Schneider of the Sicura watch firm, which kept the name alive. Schneider, head of Sicura since 1961, had guided it to success with a range of mass-market and up-market watches. Now he oversaw the absorption of the Breitling brand and principles, reintroducing the Navitimer in 1986 (when French chanteur Serge Gainsbourg could be seen wearing one). Sicura changed its name to Breitling in 1993. When Schneider died in 2015, his son Theodore succeeded him; but two years later he sold Breitling to CVC Capital Partners, ending the brand's independence. Today, the Navitimer appears in a variety of guises. The Navitimer 01 is the closest of the current range to the model's roots, but in 2009 Breitling produced a faithful reproduction of the original 806. The Navitimer continues to be an object of desire for those who are, or wish they were, pilots and racing drivers.

Rolex GMT-Master (1955)

Watches may tell stories as well as time: the circumstances in which they are worn, their previous owners, the prices they command, the people who made them and the reasons why they are made. Take, for example, one scratched, vandalized Rolex GMT-Master from the 1970s.

Rolex's GMT-Master is an outstanding example of a watchmaker getting it right first time, and in its 70 years of production it has had only one major reinvention – the GMT-Master II – and eight minor revisions. The watch owes its existence to the boom in air travel after World War Two. The war had required the creation of many new airfields, and civilian airlines were quick to grasp the potential for new business and holiday routes. Flights were no longer internal affairs but international ones, crossing borders and seas – and times zones.

It became particularly important for pilots to be able to juggle both local time and the time at their destination. Pan Am, America's largest international carrier in the twentieth century, took the initiative and approached Rolex to create a watch that could tell the time in two places simultaneously.

The GMT-Master comprised a collection of several Rolex design features, new and old. Its case was the same one used for the brand's legendary Oyster watch. It boasted a rotating bezel, which Rolex had first used on the extremely rare Zerographe model from 1937 (only 12 of these – Rolex's first to include a flyback chronograph – were made, and only four are known to survive). But the GMT-Master's bezel was divided into not 60 minutes but 24 hours, and colour-coded for day (half the bezel, in red) and night (blue) – a combination reminiscent of the colours of a well-known cola brand, and giving rise to its nickname, the 'Pepsi bezel'.

The bezel made it easy to see the time in another time zone so long as a pilot knew the time difference between it and the local time zone, as displayed by the hour, minute and second hands. The GMT-Master's great innovation, however, was the addition of a fourth central hand, which rotated 360° once every 24 hours. Reading from the fourth hand to the 24-hour bezel gave pilots a third time to refer to. Rolex was never a brand to do things by halves.

In practice, pilots usually kept the fourth hand set to Greenwich Mean Time (GMT), which was the base at the time from which all other time zones were calculated. Today that standard is known by the less-anglocentric Coordinated Universal Time (or by the abbreviation UTC); but the watch's name has stuck.

The Rolex GMT-Master, 1955, with its distinctive blue and red bezel, and innovative fourth central hand.

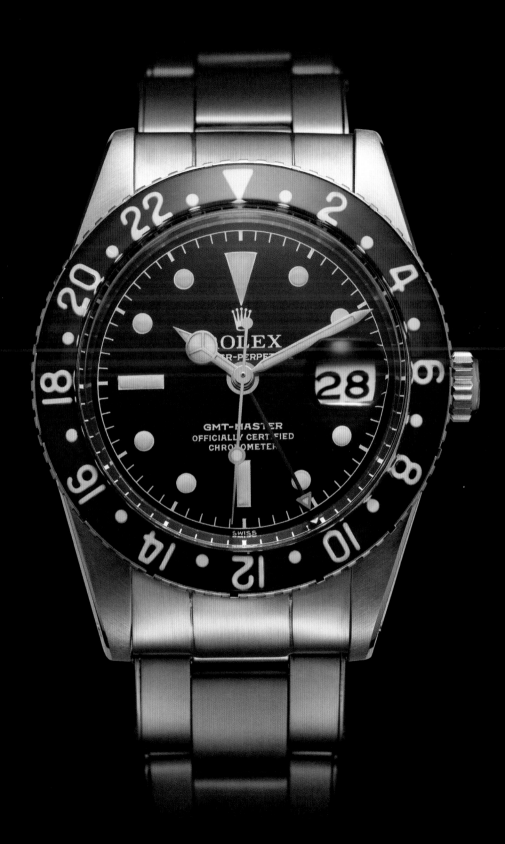

Actor Marlon Brando with the GMT-Master that he modified for his character in the film *Apocalypse Now* (1979).

On 3 October 1967, Major William J. Knight flew the experimental X-15A-2 jet at 4,520 mph (Mach 6.7), still a world record for a fixed-wing aircraft.

Another distinctive feature of the GMT-Master is the date lens, a magnifying lens built into the crystal of the watch over the date aperture. The date is the only number on the dial, which is otherwise marked by luminous batons at 6 and 9, and a triangle at 12. The bezel is luminously numbered every two hours with a triangle at midnight. It was originally made in Bakelite – but Bakelite degrades in heat and bright light such as a pilot might find above the clouds. Later versions are of aluminium; and the bezels of current GMT-Master IIs are made of a very stable ceramic material, Rolex's own, called Cerachrom.

The watch was popular from the start with pilots and other travellers. In one early marketing exercise Rolex supplied a British Army eight-man expedition called Pegasus Overland, which in 1959 circumnavigated the world and all its time zones in two off-road vehicles. William J. Knight, the pilot who still holds the record for speed in flight wore a GMT-Master as he set that record in 1967, flying an X-15 experimental plane over the Mojave desert at Mach 6.7 (4,520 mph or 7,274 km/h). Jack Swigert, commander of the ill-fated Apollo 13 space flight, wore his GMT-Master throughout the troubled mission. In the fictional world of flying, actress Honor Blackman played the part of the pilot of arch-villain Auric Goldfinger's private jet in the third James Bond film, and naturally she wore a GMT-Master.

Its popularity has ensured a healthy sellers' and collectors' market for the various incarnations of the GMT-Master. As is usual among enthusiasts, the better the condition of the watch, the higher the price it may be expected to command. There's one notable exception to this rule in the case of the GMT-Master. Twice very publicly auctioned for eye-watering prices, it has lost its bezel; and the back of the case has been very crudely scratched with a former owner's name.

The name is the key, of course, and the name is M. Brando. Marlon Brando was at the height of his powers and fame when he starred in the 1979 film *Apocalypse Now* as the rogue US Army officer Walter Kurtz. He was often a difficult performer to deal with and had frequent arguments with other actors and with the director Francis Ford Coppola. When Coppola complained to Brando that his character would not be wearing as elegant and expensive a watch as the Rolex GMT-Master, which the actor was sporting, Brando refused to take it off.

Known for his use of the highly internalized Stanislavski method of acting, Brando insisted that he and Kurtz should wear the watch in the forthcoming scene. Neither man would back down, but in a rare moment of compromise by Brando, he tore off the eye-catching Pepsi bezel so that it would not distract, as Coppola feared, from his performance.

Apocalypse Now was phenomenally successful – it won the Palme d'Or at the Cannes Film Festival before it had even been finished – and watch-observers around the world wanted to know more about Brando's. It seemed to have disappeared, and most imagined that it must have been lost during the movie's battle scenes. It finally resurfaced in 2019, at an auction by Phillips in New York. Brando had given it to his daughter Petra in 1995, as a reminder of her ability to survive whatever life could throw at her. She in turn had given it as a wedding present in 2003 to her new husband. He never wore it and kept it as Brando had left it, bezel-less and with a plain rubber strap, but otherwise in remarkably well-preserved condition.

Phillips sold Brando's modified watch for $1,952,000, enough to confirm it as a watch with a helluva story. The buyer was an Omani collector called Mohammed Zaman, who unexpectedly brought the watch back to the market only four years later, along with several other jewels of his collection. Christie's, the auction house on this occasion, initially set an estimate of $1,000,000 to $2,000,000; but such was the interest in the now iconic *Apocalypse Now* watch that, ahead of sale day, it revised that to between $4,205,000 and $7,288,000. Christie's knows its business – on the day it was bought for $5,124,783. The new owner, the latest chapter in this watch's story, remains for the time being unknown.

Omega Speedmaster Professional (1957)

Watches are tested to great depths, to great heights, at extremes of temperature and pressure, all in the name of reliability. If there's one environment where reliability is absolutely critical, it's in space. Only two watches have definitely been to the Moon; and only the Omega Speedmaster was there on official business.

You can't buy any of the Omega Speedmasters that went into space. They were government property and had to be returned on completion of each mission. In practice, however, many of the astronauts on the Apollo Moon missions took their own personal watches as well as the Speedmasters that were the program's official timepieces. In almost all cases there is no evidence to confirm whether any of these private possessions made it to the Moon's surface.

Before the space missions, no watch had been designed to travel through space. The Omega Speedmaster was one of a trio of watches launched by Omega in 1957, aimed at more terrestrial pursuits. All derived from the firm's Seamaster; the most obvious member of the Class of '57 was the Seamaster 300 (see page 58), intended to compete with Blancpain's Fifty Fathoms (see page 70) and the Rolex Submariner (see page 74). Alongside it was the

Railmaster, originally aimed at railway workers and others who worked near magnetic fields. It was anti-magnetic – railroads depended on keeping to timetables, and unprotected watches were vulnerable to the waves generated by the telegraph lines that ran alongside almost all rail routes. It became popular with engineers and scientists in many fields.

The Speedmaster was for racing enthusiasts, and unlike its fellow newbies it included a chronograph function. It was not the first watch to do so, but by moving the tachymeter scale to the bezel, Omega made the main dial and sub-dials much easier to read. The design went through several small adjustments in the early years of its production, and in 1962, the latest version was the Speedmaster 2998, the watch worn by Wally Schirra as he orbited the Earth six times on 3 October as part of NASA's Project Mercury. NASA had not yet selected the Speedmaster as an official piece of kit, and Schirra's flight with his own personal watch went a long way to demonstrating its suitability for space travel, something even Omega did not have the resources to do. It performed without a hitch.

Omega did, however, bring out three new variations of the Speedy (as it is known) that year. Unknown to Omega, or to Longines, Breitling, Rolex and other manufacturers, NASA put the Speedmaster

The Omega Speedmaster, launched in 1957 alongside the Railmaster and the Seamaster 300.

Astronaut Buzz Aldrin inside the Apollo 11 kunar module on 20 July 1969 with the NASA-issue Speedmaster Professional, which he wore when he walked on the Moon.

The Silver Snoopy Award, given to Omega after the ill-fated Apollo 13 mission, engraved on the back of an Omega Speedmaster.

105.003 and several other watches through a series of endurance tests designed to recreate the harsh extremes of space. Only the Speedy survived.

These were secret trials, and the first that Omega knew of its success was when TV pictures showed astronaut Ed White taking America's first spacewalk in June 1965, with a Speedmaster on his wrist. Thereafter, Omega worked with NASA on further developments and refinements, which culminated in the 105.012, a new version with crown guards and a wider, asymmetric dial. It was renamed the Speedmaster Professional, but it's the watch known by everyone today as the Moonwatch.

Apollo 11 took off from the Kennedy Space Center in Florida on 16 July 1969. It was the culmination of all the space flights that had gone before, the mission which would for the first time land a human being on the Moon. Its crew – Neil Armstrong, Buzz Aldrin and Michael Collins – all wore Speedmaster Professionals as they orbited around the Moon. As Collins piloted the Command Module in orbit around the Moon, Armstrong and Aldrin prepared to make their descent to the surface in the Lunar Landing Module. At the last minute, a failed electronic timer on board the Command Module meant that Armstrong had to leave his Speedy with Collins as a back-up to Collins' own; so although Armstrong, as commander of the mission, was the first man to walk on the Moon, Aldrin was the first to do so with a watch – the Omega Speedmaster Professional.

The success of the Apollo program is regularly cited as humankind's single greatest achievement. After 10 years of trials, triumphs and disasters, human beings made the first voyages beyond our planet's atmosphere to another object in space. No one can take those achievements away from Armstrong, Aldrin, Collins, NASA and indeed Omega. On their return to Earth, however, the astronauts' watches were taken from them and put into storage. Speedmasters accompanied every subsequent manned flight to the Moon. Only one experienced any kind of failure: Dave Scott, commander of the Apollo 15 voyage, noticed on his return to the lunar module after a period of 'extra-vehicular activity' – a drive on the Moon in the new Lunar Rover – that the crystal had gone from his Speedmaster. It must have popped off at some point during the drive.

The Moonwatch also played its part in the successful return of the greatest failure of the Apollo program. When Apollo 13 had to abort its mission because of a ruptured oxygen tank, air supply and power for the onboard electronics ran dangerously low. Commander Jim Lovell's Speedy was the crew's only way of timing to perfection the firing of the re-entry rockets. The resulting correction of their course made the difference between successfully re-entering the Earth's atmosphere and burning up in the attempt. If timing is everything, it was never more so than in that moment.

In recognition of Omega's contribution to the Moon program, and to the successful failure that was Apollo 13, NASA presented the company with a Silver Snoopy Award in 1970. This internal award was devised as a way of promoting an awareness among NASA employees and contractors of their role in the safety of the astronauts who depended on them. Charles Schulz, the artist behind the popular Snoopy cartoon series, gave his services freely in the design of the award, which takes the form of a silver brooch depicting Snoopy the dog as an astronaut. Since the award's introduction in 1968, it has been given to more than 15,000 individuals and companies. Although the design and name of the award are intended to be light-hearted, the Silver Snoopy is one of the highest internal honours which NASA can bestow, awarded on average to fewer than 1 per cent of its nominees. Omega's well-deserved pin is now displayed in the Omega Museum in Switzerland.

Junghans Max Bill (1961)

In a world where watches have calendars, timers, tachymeters, alarms, chimes, countdowns, count-ups, sun-ups, sunsets, lunar cycles, moisture sensors, multi-coloured dials and bezels, most people just want a watch that tells the time. As a simple watch, Junghans Max Bill fits the bill.

Junghans is a German company, based in the Black Forest, an area famed for its folk-art wooden cuckoo clocks. Founded in 1861 by brothers-in-law Erhard Junghans and Jakob Zeller-Tobler, the firm started out carving the wooden elements of the clocks, which were popular souvenirs for European tourists. They featured dancing figures or whistling birds that appeared every hour, often with musical chimes and Junghans & Tobler, as they were known, made the cases, decorative elements, hands and pendulums for them.

The Junghans range expanded to include metal clock parts, and in 1866 it offered its first pocket watches. Erhard Junghans died soon afterwards, but his wife took over the running of the company, and in time her sons Arthur and Erhard Jr took over from her. Arthur visited the United States and studied the mass production techniques being practised there. Bringing these processes back to

Germany he was able to make watches faster and cheaper than before, and the company went from strength to strength.

By the end of the nineteenth century, its 3,000 employees were manufacturing three million watches a year in the largest watch factory in the world. In 1918, it built an even larger one on the steep slopes of the Lauterbach valley. Good light was vital in the assembly of tiny watch parts, and hard to find in the deep, darkly wooded valleys of the Black Forest. Junghans overcame the problem with a factory which was effectively a series of nine long terraced production rooms, each higher and set back further against the hillside than the one below it. In this way every workbench could be by a window. It was an innovative solution, and the factory still stands today, its architecture the subject of protected status, housing the Junghans World Museum.

As a German company, Junghans was naturally chosen to supply cockpit clocks to the German air force, the Luftwaffe, during World War Two. Germany's military forces were disbanded at the end of the conflict, but in West Germany they were reconstituted in 1955 as the Bundeswehr when the rapid remilitarization of East Germany became a concern. Junghans successfully won the contract to supply the new air

Simplicity itself – a 1960s edition of the Junghans Max Bill watch, named after its Swiss designer.

Max Bill (1908–94) at work in 1960. In the 1920s he studied at the Bauhaus under Wassily Kandinsky (1866–1944), Paul Klee (1879–1940) and Oskar Schlemmer (1888–1943).

A 1958 version of Max Bill's elegant Junghans kitchen clock with its built-in timer, originally designed for Junghans in 1956.

force with a pilot's wristwatch, which remains a well-regarded specialized watch today.

After Arthur Junghans returned from America in 1903, the company's output was eminently practical and functional in concept. A collaboration with one of the great designers of the Bauhaus School of industrial design was therefore an obvious development. The philosophy of the Bauhaus can be summarized in the dictum 'Form follows function'. Since natural forms have evolved to be perfectly adapted for their needs and functions, so manmade objects should focus on their intended uses and be designed accordingly, often starting with the simplest geometric shapes. In architectural terms Junghans' terraced factory was a perfect example.

In the late 1950s, Junghans approached the Swiss graphic designer Max Bill, a former student at the Bauhaus, to design some timepieces for the company. His first effort is now hailed as a design classic – a kitchen clock with a clockwork timer, both built into a simple shape like an inverted teardrop.

Bill delivered his first wristwatch for Junghans in 1961. It was beautiful. It carried the minimum of marks on its dial, in fine lines black on white, giving an impression of space and calmness. There was a single scale of 60 divisions, using batons without any accompanying circles, twice as long at the hours as elsewhere, with the minutes numbered at multiples of five outside the index and a full set of the hours closer to the centre, all in a small but clear typeface designed by Bill himself. That was all – no sub-dials, no chronometer buttons, no bezel, no luminosity. The hands were simple sticks and they pointed out the time.

It was a long way from the ornate, folksy Black Forest clocks that started it all, but very much in line with the wristwatches that Junghans first started making in 1926 – when it was an early adopter of the novelty of luminosity. After some initial attempts to follow fashion with some octagonal or rectangular cases, and at least one example with a lattice guard across the crystal, Junghans wristwatches settled on simple circular dials, with large Arabic numerals and the characteristic unadorned scale of batons which Max Bill adopted and refined.

The relationship was a good one, and Bill worked closely with the company for many years. The Junghans Max Bill is central to the company's continuing survival and although it has on occasion been given complications such as a date or a chronograph, it remains true to the spacious ethic of its first incarnation. It is now available with manual, automatic and even quartz movements, and with or without hour indices. Although most of the present range are 38mm in diameter, one version clocks in at the Max Bill's original 34mm.

Max Bill died in 1994, and the home that he designed and built himself in Zurich according to his Bauhaus principles is now the museum and offices of the Max Bill Georges Vantongerloo Foundation, established by Bill's widow Angela – Vantongerloo was a Belgian artist of the De Stijl school, whose legacy Bill admired and promoted. A separate Max Bill Foundation, established by Max's son Jakob, preserves and promotes Max Bill's own legacy. Ownership of Junghans has long since passed out of the Junghans family and the company has changed hands many times. But, now more than 160 years old, its own legacy shows no sign of being lost. People will always want to simply tell the time.

'[Max Bill] delivered his first wristwatch for Junghans in 1961. It was beautiful. It carried the minimum of marks on its dial, in fine lines black on white, giving an impression of space and calmness.'

Seiko Quartz-Astron 35SQ (1969)

The history of horology is divided into before and after the Astron. It's the watch that precipitated the Quartz Crisis and changed the traditional watch industry forever. Yet nobody can say the signs weren't there, and nobody can blame Seiko for winning a race in which many others were participants.

Seiko launched the Astron 35SQ in Tokyo on Christmas morning, 1969. It was relatively expensive for a watch, the price of a mid-range family car then, the equivalent of $10,000 now. It had a sleek, cushion-shaped case of brushed gold into which the crown was set so as not to break the understated elegance of the gently curving sides. It had no extra complications – no calendar, no chronometer, not even any numerals – just three hands, batons for the hours and a double baton at 12 o'clock. It was stylish, not flashy – and Seiko sold 100 of them before the year was out.

The gold case was not the attraction. Nor, really, was the claimed accuracy – plus or minus five seconds a month was better than any other watch could boast in a day, but (as the *New York Times* mockingly reported a week later) 'If you're one of those rare persons who must be accurate within five seconds a month, the Japanese have a wristwatch for you'. It was the technology – the Astron was the world's first quartz wristwatch and, as Seiko presciently declared in the advertising copy for it, 'Someday, all watches will be made this way'.

Seiko had spent a decade perfecting the technology, which stemmed from the discovery that a quartz crystal oscillates at a given rate when a given electrical current is passed through it. In the 1969 Astron, that rate was 8,192Hz: 8,192 times a second. Compare that with a mechanical watch, in which the balance wheel spins back and forth at 4Hz. If one of those four oscillations is disturbed, it can affect the watch's timing by up to a quarter of a second per second. If one of the quartz crystal's 8,192 oscillations is out, who's going to notice? As a side note, modern quartz watches now work on 32,768Hz: four times the speed and accuracy of the first Astron and 8,000 times faster than a mechanical movement.

The Quartz-Astron should have put Seiko in a dominant position within the industry for years to come, and the company certainly reaped the immediate benefits of its breakthrough. But in an extraordinary act of generosity, Seiko placed its patents in the public domain. Now anyone could make a quartz watch – and almost everyone did. As costs came down and mass production went up, it

A 1969 edition Seiko Quartz-Astron 35SQ. The world's first quartz watch, it changed the watch industry forever.

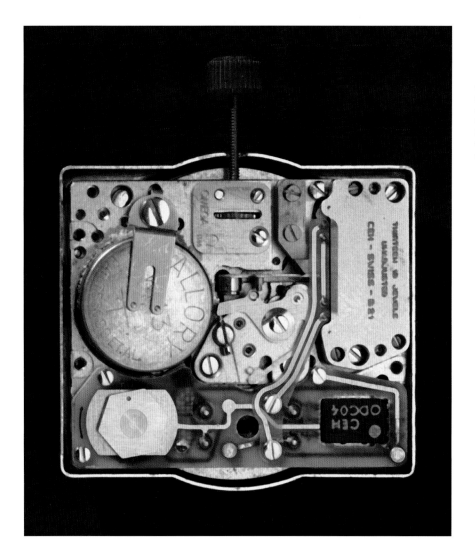

Omega's Beta 21, one of a series of experimental quartz movements produced by Switzerland's Centre Électronique Horloger in the race to create the first quartz wristwatch.

Hamilton's stylish Ventura wristwatch, launched in 1957, was the world's first battery-powered watch.

seemed that a cheap, reliable quartz wristwatch was within everyone's reach.

This was the real revolution, the real earthquake to hit the traditional watchmakers of the world, and it unfolded not at once but over the next few years. Sales of watches with mechanical movements collapsed because the old firms could not compete on price, accuracy or even looks – the Astron was a handsome piece, after all. When digital watches made their debut, it was game over – the Seiko 06LC, the first digital watch to display the time to six digits (hours, minutes and seconds), was launched in 1973. In the Swiss watch industry, between 1970 and 1983, the number of individual firms fell from 1,600 to 600. The number of employees, 90,000 in 1970, had fallen to 28,000 by 1988.

And yet electrical clocks and watches were nothing new. The piezo-electric aspect of quartz was discovered in 1880, by Marie Curie's husband Pierre and his brother Jacques. The first quartz clock was built by Warren Marrison and J.W. Horton in the research laboratories of Bell Telephone in 1927. The Ventura watch launched by Hamilton in 1957, with its futuristic curve-sided triangular dial looking like a prop from sci-fi TV series *Star Trek*, was the world's first battery-powered watch, 22 years ahead of the Astron.

Although Switzerland is often portrayed as having been caught out by Seiko, it is simply not true. Seiko unveiled a prototype of the Astron in 1967, the same year in which a consortium of 20 Swiss manufacturers, formed in 1962 as the Centre Électronique Horloger (CEH): the Electronic Watch Centre, exhibited its own prototype quartz movement, the Beta 1. Switzerland and Seiko were neck and neck.

The CEH consisted of some of the major players in the Swiss industry – Omega, Rolex, Patek Philippe, IWC, Piaget, Longines, Rado and others – and while they shared some technology, they were vying with each other to get their own production models into the market. Omega won that internal race: its Electroquartz watch, using a Beta 21 movement, arrived in shops only four months after the Astron.

Swiss quartz watches achieved the same standard of accuracy as Seiko's, but they hadn't mastered electronic miniaturization the way the Japanese had. Swiss quartz movements were bulky, and they drained their batteries much quicker than the Astron did. Seiko had won not only the race but also the technology war. Being first is everything, and for years to come, quartz timekeeping would be identified with modern Japanese thinking and not traditional Swiss quality.

Watch snobs looked down on quartz, but the crisis was real and, unable to compete on price, Switzerland's way through was to go up-market. The emergence of the luxury watch market dates from this time and it has been the saving of the Swiss horological economy. It is not yet true that 'all watches are made this way', but with even high-end Swiss watches now available in quartz versions, only a fool would rule it out.

'But in an extraordinary act of generosity, Seiko placed its patents in the public domain. Now anyone could make a quartz watch – and almost everyone did.'

Heuer Monaco (1969)

The world had seen square watches before 1969, and of course it had seen chronographs. The combination of the two, however, was startling and exciting, especially when associated with the power and machismo of Formula One motor racing. Add a Hollywood superstar into the mix, and Heuer had a hit.

Edouard Heuer founded the Heuer Watchmaking Company in Switzerland in 1860. His great-grandson Jack Heuer is a chairman of the company today, albeit in an honorary capacity – the company has changed hands many times since the Quartz Crisis. From its inception Heuer developed a particular interest in chronographs. Edouard Heuer made his first one in 1882 and patented an oscillating pinion in 1887, which is still at the heart of many mechanical timers even today.

Early in the history of the motor car, and even earlier in the history of motor racing, Heuer was granted a patent for its dashboard timer, the Time Of Trip. In the days before seconds counted quite as much as now, the Time Of Trip was an ordinary clock showing the time in hours and minutes, with a sub-dial at 12 o'clock indicating the time elapsed since the start of the journey. A crown at the top adjusted the real time, and a single button worked to start, stop and reset the timer.

Charles-Auguste Heuer, son of the founder, launched two ground-breaking stopwatches in 1916. The Semikrograph was accurate to 0.02 seconds and had a split-second function for showing the difference in time between two neck-and-neck competitors. The Mikrograph was the first timer in the world to measure time to the nearest one-hundredth, 0.01, of a second. In 1933, the company brought out a successor to the Time Of Trip, the Autavia, for use in cars and that still novel form of transport (at the time), aeroplanes. The name was transferred in the 1960s to a line of wristwatches. During World War Two, Heuer supplied instruments to the Luftwaffe.

After the war the company turned its attention to sports of all kinds. The Auto-Graph was aimed at rally drivers and had a bezel tachymeter with which a driver or their navigator could check that they were achieving their planned pace over a given mile. The device could also be used, according to its advertising copy, to keep track of golf scores. The Mareographe had sophisticated colour-coded complications that could indicate the state of the tides for sailors, a function easily adapted to follow the phases of the Moon. Both these watches were originally produced for the New York outfitter Abercrombie & Fitch.

At the same time Heuer developed timing systems for sports organizers at racing events of all kinds including skiing and – naturally – motor

The Heuer Monaco 1133 B Steve McQueen, made famous by appearing on the actor's wrist in the motor racing film *Le Mans* (1971).

Actor Steve McQueen (1930–80) in the film *Le Mans*, wearing the racing overalls of his friend Jo Siffert and the watch which now bears his name.

The Heuer Monaco 1133 B comes in a racing-themed box.

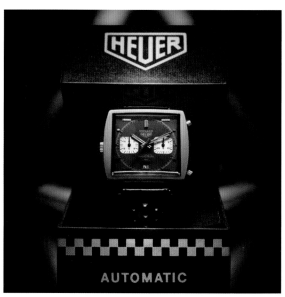

racing. In a different sort of race, astronaut John Glenn wore a Heuer chronograph, the first watch in space, as a back-up to the inboard instruments of his Mercury-Atlas 6 spacecraft during the first US manned flight around the Earth in 1962.

Heuer was involved in a race of another kind in the 1960s. Competing with Seiko and Zenith, Heuer teamed up with Hamilton and Breitling in an attempt to produce the world's first automatic chronographs. The results were launched in a lavish press conference in New York on 3 March 1969, where Heuer unveiled automatic versions of its two existing models – the Autavia and the Carrera – and a brand new watch, the like of which had never been seen before. It was big, it was square, it was the Monaco.

These first automatic chronographs used Heuer's new Calibre 11 movement and were advertised and badged under the name Chrono-Matic. Zenith didn't enter the market until later in 1969; Seiko finally came to the table a year later.

The Monaco had to be seen to be believed. Yes, the hands went round inside a circular register divided into quarter-seconds – but that circle was framed in a square window. Yes, that square frame had straight top and bottom edges – but its sides were gracefully convex. Yes, there was a crown on the side – but it was on the *left* side, leaving the right free for the chronometer function buttons. After all, here was a watch that did not need to be wound.

There were two sub-dials within the round register, white within blue; naturally they were square, but with softer, rounded corners. And the hours indices were not numerals but horizontal batons, reminiscent of a car passing at speed, and elongated to extraordinary effect at 1, 5, 7 and 11. Even the hands were bold – broad blades bi-coloured in red and white, like racing colours. Finally, it had a date aperture at 6 o'clock and was water-resistant to 100m (328ft). It was a surprising watch.

The Monaco was the brainchild of Jack Heuer, Edouard's great-grandson, who was determined to make a bigger splash with Heuer's new automatic movement than by simply inserting it into existing designs. He acquired exclusive rights to a new case designed by Swiss manufacturer Ervin Piquerez – the world's first water-resistant square case. It was a fitting housing for the new Calibre 11 – unlike the Carrera, which had to be replaced with a larger one to accommodate the automatic movement.

The Monaco made an immediate impact in 1969. But it made an even bigger one in 1971, thanks to a chain of happy coincidences. Firstly, Heuer wanted to expand its profile in the motor racing community and sponsored Swiss Formula One driver Jo Siffert as an ambassador for the brand. Siffert therefore wore Heuer logos on his clothing and his car.

Secondly, Siffert was a friend of Hollywood bad boy Steve McQueen, then at the height of his popularity and known for daring vehicle sequences in many of his films – the motorbike pursuit in *The Great Escape* (1963), the 11-minute car chase in *Bullitt* (1968). McQueen had been bitterly disappointed not to be cast in John Frankenheimer's 1966 film about the racing world, *Grand Prix*, and in 1970 he made his own motor movie, *Le Mans*, about the annual 24-hour race at the Le Mans circuit in France.

Siffert rented racing cars from his own collection to the production company for *Le Mans*, and also lent McQueen his own racing suit, complete with its Heuer branding. McQueen, who filmed during the actual Le Mans event for greater reality, decided that for complete verisimilitude his character should wear a Monaco – and the extraordinary watch is very visible on McQueen's wrist in many of the movie's scenes. The sight of the big square watch on the superstar was more valuable to Heuer than any number of ambassadors, and the Monaco remains at the core of the company's output today.

The film was released in June 1971. The success of the film, and of the Monaco's exposure in it, was tempered by Siffert's death only four months later. He died in a crash at the Brands Hatch circuit in England, where he had won his first Grand Prix only three years earlier. McQueen, who died in 1980, owned two Monacos: one was sold in Hollywood in 2016 for $650,000; the other came under the hammer in 2020 for 10 times the auctioneer's estimate: $2.2 million.

Audemars Piguet Royal Oak (1972)

Sports watches used to be for people who played sports. That all changed in 1972 when a watchmaker responded to the influx of cheap quartz watches from Japan by making a watch so expensive that no one in their right mind would wear it on a playing field.

Audemars Piguet was founded in 1881 by two childhood friends, Jules Louis Audemars and Edward Auguste Piguet, who met again in their twenties and realized they shared a passion for watchmaking. Audemars had been making movements for Tiffany & Co, and Piguet's speciality was the skilled work of adjusting movements so that they kept good time.

Theirs was a modest operation. The company had grown sufficiently by 1907 to force them to move into larger premises, to accommodate their 10 employees. By the 1950s, the workforce had grown to 30, but mass production was not the Audemars Piguet way – between 1930 and 1962 it made a total of 307 watches, so few that it didn't even bother to give them serial numbers.

As the Quartz Crisis hit at the end of the 1960s, other manufacturers might have had strength in depth, with established models and brand names; Audemars Piguet did not. It had to do something radical or face almost certain collapse. Recent market research from Italy – home of Ferrari, Alfa Romeo, Maserati and Lamborghini – suggested a possible opportunity to the company's managing director at the time, Georges Golay.

On the eve of the annual watchmakers' showcase Baselworld in 1971, Golay rang Gérald Genta, a designer then at the peak of his powers, who had previously created Omega's Constellation model and Patek Philippe's Golden Ellipse. 'I need a design for a high-end steel sports watch of unprecedented finish and beauty,' he said (or something along those lines). 'And I need it by tomorrow morning.' It was 4.00 p.m.

'Challenge accepted,' replied Genta (or something along those lines); and remarkably, by the end of the night, he presented Golay with sketches of the watch of his dreams. Inspired by the faceplate of an old-fashioned diving helmet, the bezel was octagonal with eight visible hexagonal screwheads countersunk into it at the corners, and a hexagonal crown. The strap was to be a linked bracelet, tapering from the case to the clasp like the scales on the tail of a fish. There were no numerals, and no second hand – just a minimalist scale of 60 divisions and broad batons for the hours, with a date aperture at 3 o'clock.

None of the watch's distinguishing characteristics were easy to manufacture as none

Audemars Piguet's Royal Oak watch, featuring Gérald Genta's trademark octagonal porthole design.

The incident from which the Royal Oak gets its name: King Charles II of Britain hides in a tree from the forces of republicanism while a family of royalists deny any knowledge of his whereabouts, in an engraving by John Leech from Gilbert Beckett's *Comic History of England* (1850).

The eighth and latest Royal Navy battleship to be given the name HMS *Royal Oak*, launched in 1914 and sunk by a German torpedo in Scapa Flow in 1939.

were circular. The bracelet alone – because of its narrowing design – had 154 components (128 of them different from each other) and it had to be assembled and decorated entirely by hand. The quality of steel which Genta specified for the new watch's case was so high that the first prototypes were made of white gold, because it was cheaper and easier to machine.

It was to be 39mm in diameter, relatively large at the time. The overall depth of the watch would be only 7mm, containing Audemars Piguet's finest movement, the Calibre 2121, which was only 3.05mm deep. The company had form for producing thin watches: in 1946 it created a movement a mere 1.64mm from top to bottom.

Presented with such demanding specifications, the firm's staff and contractors spent a difficult year resolving them into the finished product. Nevertheless, Georges Golay was able to launch the new watch at Baselworld 1972, a year to the day after Gérald Genta designed it. It needed a name and, because of the naval inspiration behind it, it was christened the Royal Oak, after the most prestigious name ever given to a British warship.

In fact there have been eight HMS *Royal Oaks* in the British navy's history, all themselves named after a celebrated tree in which the future King Charles II hid to escape his enemies during the English Civil War in 1651. Perhaps Golay was hoping that his Royal Oak would be the means of his own escape from the Quartz Crisis. If so, he may have been disappointed that year. The Royal Oak was met with interest, even curiosity, but far from universal admiration. Its appearance was unfashionable, even ugly to the onlookers of the time; and its price, coming from a relatively small operator in the industry, was eye watering. At 3,300 Swiss francs (£2,850), the steel monstrosity was more expensive than a gold dress watch from Patek Philippe, and 10 times more expensive than Rolex's Submariner. The consensus was that Audemars Piguet had overreached and would be bankrupt within a matter of months.

It took more than a year for the first 1,000 Royal Oaks to be sold – but, oh, how sought after are those first 1,000 now. The second 1,000 took rather less, and the third and fourth less still. By the end of the 1970s, the Royal Oak was proved to have shown the way forward for the beleaguered Swiss watch industry. In its wake, the expensive luxury sports watch has been the saviour of all the companies that were still in business at the end of the crisis.

Like all iconic watches, the Royal Oak has seen its share of upgrades and updates. It got its second hand eventually; and the 1981 Royal Oak Perpetual Calendar – the thinnest of its kind, of course – is so mechanically perfect that it will not need to be reset until the year 2100. Among the Royal Oak's contemporary admirers are actor Arnold Schwarzenegger, racing driver Michael Schumacher and rapper Jay-Z – all men who know a thing or two about survival. Basketball player LeBron James, the NBA's all-time highest scorer and a man for whom accuracy is everything, is also a fan. Gérald Genta, who went on to design other iconic watches including the Patek Philippe Nautilus, regarded the Royal Oak as his finest hour.

'It needed a name and, because of the naval inspiration behind it, it was christened the Royal Oak, after the most prestigious name ever given to a British warship.'

Seiko 06LC (1973)

When 'The Most Beautiful Woman in the World' met 'El Commandante', sparks flew. The latter was so impressed with the former that he took the watch from his wrist and gave it to her. She kept it until her death in 2023; and there was considerable excitement when it was auctioned a year later.

Gina Lollobrigida was one of the great European stars of the golden age of Hollywood. Italian by birth, her talent, beauty and what was then called 'sex appeal' quickly caught international attention. She worked with some of the great directors of the 1950s and 1960s, including King Vidor, Carol Reed, John Huston and Billy Wilder; and she starred opposite all the most famous male leads of the day, among them Humphrey Bogart, Tony Curtis, Burt Lancaster, Errol Flynn, Anthony Quinn, Yul Brynner, Rock Hudson, Sean Connery and Alec Guinness. Her leading role in the 1955 Italian rom-com *La Donna Più Bella del Mondo* (The Most Beautiful Woman in the World), provided a soubriquet that admiring cinema-goers were only too ready to use.

But Hollywood is fickle, and by the 1970s her silver-screen star was waning. As the roles began to dry up, Lollobrigida began a second career as a photojournalist, taking advantage of her Hollywood connections to post stories and pictures of Paul Newman, Audrey Hepburn and other stars. She showed genuine talent for her new role and was soon photographing great figures in other spheres, such as politician Henry Kissinger, artist Salvador Dalí, singer Ella Fitzgerald and – memorably – the German football team.

The high point of her journalistic career, as far as she was concerned, was the interview that she secured in 1974 with 'El Commandante' – the then prime minister of Cuba, Fidel Castro. Marxist Castro was a thorn in the side of the United States, for whom the proximity of communist Cuba was a serious threat. The fiasco of the failed US invasion of Cuba at the Bay of Pigs in 1961, the nuclear fears triggered by the Cuban Missile Crisis of 1962 and several American attempts to assassinate the Cuban leader, had taught Castro to avoid contact with Western journalists.

As a European, however, Lollobrigida was less interested in his politics than in his qualities as a man; and when he understood that, he agreed to meet her. Some say he went so far as to request the interview himself during a visit to Italy, although Lollobrigida claimed that she wrote to him while in Moscow photographing the Russian poet Yevgeny Yevtushenko. Whatever the truth, she rushed to Cuba within four days of hearing from him, taking little more than 'eight

The Seiko 06LC 0614 5010T quartz digital watch that Fidel Castro gave to Gina Lollobrigida in 1974, engraved with his name and admiration for her.

Cuban prime minister Fidel Castro, photographed during an interview with American journalists in Havana on 29 September 1974, only a few days after his meeting with Gina Lollobrigida.

After a showing of her documentary film *Portrait of Fidel Castro* during the Berlin International Film Festival on 30 June 1975, Lollobrigida signs autographs with one hand while wearing Castro's watch on the other.

cameras, 200 rolls of film, 10 pairs of new blue jeans, a sound technician, a cameraman and a US girlfriend.'

She spent 10 days in Cuba, photographing Castro in several locations and asking him both political and personal questions. What was the future of the Revolution? And was he married? 'I am not familiar with the statistics on married and single chiefs of state,' he replied, 'but I assure you that women occupy a very important place in my life and in my feelings.' Lollobrigida was impressed by him, and by the warmth of affection from the Cuban people toward him.

Rumours abound that Lollobrigida and Castro did more than simply talk together, and Humphrey Bogart once said she 'made Marilyn Monroe look like Shirley Temple'. There is no evidence that they were more than cordial with each other. But at their parting, in a very personal gesture, Castro took off the watch that he was wearing and gave it to Lollobrigida. Later he arranged to have it inscribed, 'A Gina, con ammirazione' – *with admiration* – 'Fidel Castro'. And what was this special watch? Was it a high-priced import from the decadent capitalist West, laden with dials and sub-dials? Was it a rather imperfect imitation of such a watch from one of his communist allies? Was it a simple watch as would befit a man of the people?

Yes and no. It was, appropriately, a revolutionary watch. It was a plain watch, with the sort of display of hours, minutes and seconds that nowadays millions of ordinary people wear without a thought. It was certainly an import, and one that was very expensive in its day. And it was the scourge of the decadent capitalist Swiss watch industry.

Fidel Castro wore a Seiko 06LC. LC stands for Liquid Crystal, and the 06 signified that this was the first watch in the world to carry a six-figure digital liquid crystal display – hours, minutes and seconds. Commonplace today, it was a ground-breaking development when it was launched in October 1973. Quartz-powered watches with analogue dials had been shaking up the traditional watch industry for the best part of a decade, but this new digital display was the result of research and invention by Epson, now best known for its home and office computer printers. It boasted a life of 50,000 hours, and although the watch was launched with some trepidation about the reliability of this brand-new technology, it is said that not a single example was returned for the failure of the display.

The 06LC went through several iterations. Its Seiko model number was 0614 50xx; 0614 was the Seiko quartz movement which drove it, which was accurate to +/– 10 seconds a month. The number 5000 signified the styling of the case when it was first released. Castro's was a 5010, with a slightly squarer case; and there was a later 5020 too. Most were cased in steel, but Castro's 06LC was an 0614 5010T, with a top-of-the-range T-for-titanium case and bracelet.

Lollobrigida's effects were sold at the Wannenes auction house in Genoa, northern Italy, over two days in May 2024. Castro's watch was, rather surprisingly, put up without a reserve. Without the engraved evidence of Fidel's affection for Gina, Seiko 06LCs can be had for around $3,000. With Castro's admiration so indelibly expressed, however, Gina Lollobrigida's gift was sold for $20,365.

'At their parting, in a very personal gesture, Castro took off the watch that he was wearing and gave it to Lollobrigida.'

Hewlett-Packard HP-01 (1977)

Although it was produced for only two years, Hewlett-Packard's one and only watch made many friends and is regarded with affection by collectors. Before the internet ruled our lives, it was, it is often argued, the world's first smartwatch.

Bill Hewlett and David Packard, two electrical engineering graduates, set up their company in 1939, producing electronic testing and measuring equipment. Their start-up costs amounted to $538, which had to cover the rental of a one-car lock-up in Palo Alto, California. At the end of their first year of trading they had sold $5,369 of goods for a profit of $1,563, and they built the company from there. Their move into calculators saw the introduction of the Hewlett-Packard 9100A in 1968, a powerful desktop machine with scientific functions and memory that some cite as the world's first home computer.

One of their employees in the early 1970s was Steve Wozniak, who was developing, in his spare time, the first iteration of the Apple computer. HP had first refusal on innovations conceived by its staff – and turned down Wozniak's offer of Apple five times before he took 'No' for an answer and threw in his lot with Steve Jobs. HP had introduced its own line of desktop computers, the 9800 series, in 1971.

The HP-01 was not the first calculator watch. Pulsar and Calcron had both debuted versions in

1975, and perhaps their arrival stung Hewlett-Packard into action. When HP's reply appeared in 1977, it knocked the earlier watches into a cocked hat. The HP-01 was a scientific wonder capable of complex calculations of time, speed, distance and cost far beyond the basic mathematical functions of its 1975 arrivals. Advertisements for it pointed out that 'with the HP-01, you can compute and then count down the time it takes for a command to reach a spacecraft several hundred million miles away'.

Naturally it had all the complications of a mere watch as well – countdown, alarm, stopwatch, 200-year calendar – but it was its ability to use data from all these functions with its calculator that made the HP-01 rather special. It even had a memory that could pull up phone numbers along with reminders to make the call.

Combining all these clever things in a wristwatch was far from easy. The HP-01 was a big watch, even by the standards of the emerging luxury sports market. Its giant brain was contained in a steel case measuring 45 x 40 x 15mm and weighing in at 170g (6oz), significantly more than twice the weight of a Rolex Submariner, for example. Nevertheless, it was a marvel of miniaturization, with its cheerful red seven-digit LED display and its 28 keys arranged in four rows. Inside, beside the circuitry, were the

The LED dispay and tiny keyboard of an early edition Hewlett Packard HP-01, the world's first smartwatch.

A Hewlett Packard HP-01 in its presentation case, with stylus and instruction manual.

Twenty-one years after the HP-01, Seiko developer Kazuhiro Koyama wears the Ruputer, the world's first wristwatch computer, with its miniature orange joystick.

three batteries required to keep it running with an accuracy of +/– 30 seconds a year – good for its period, and not bad compared to the +/– 15 seconds of today's quartz watches.

The keypad was undeniably hard to use for the fat-fingered. Six basic keys stood proud of the surface, but the rest – to prevent accidental keying – were sunk below. To press them, HP provided a neat little stylus which was stored in the clasp of the bracelet. Anticipating that this could easily be lost in the field, HP also included a double-ended biro-stylus in the presentation box.

The HP-01 was Hewlett-Packard's first calculator to use algebraic sequencing for its calculations. Previous models had all used a system called Reverse Polish Notation, which placed the mathematical operation after the numbers involved. So, for example, calculating 2 plus 3 involved typing '2 3 +'. Algebraic order, '2 + 3', was a more logical, more human way of expressing the calculation.

It was a powerful, clever little package. But its timing was wrong. Light-emitting diodes (LEDs) were already beginning to give way to liquid-crystal displays (LCDs) – a change illustrated, as ever, by James Bond. In *Live and Let Die*, Roger Moore's first appearance in the role in 1973, he wore a state-of-the-art Hamilton Pulsar P2 LED watch. By 1977, when the HP-01 appeared, Moore was sporting a Seiko DK001 LCD model in the latest Bond film, *The Spy Who Loved Me*.

Hewlett-Packard was already producing desktop machines with the same functions as the HP-01, but with full-sized buttons. Obviously, they were just as likely to be on hand for the target market as a wristwatch.

Too late with its LEDs, the HP-01 was ahead of its time as a smartwatch. Miniaturization had not yet caught up with Hewlett-Packard's ambitions. When it did, in 1998, Seiko's Ruputer watch was the first practical result. The Ruputer had a 102 x 64-pixel LCD screen capable of displaying graphics as well as alpha-numerical characters. Data could be entered into its memory with a tiny joystick built into the case below the display – a time-consuming process akin to entering one's initials into the High Score league in an arcade video game – or by connection to a home computer. Software developers could write new programs for the watch in C language.

The Ruputer had its own limitations. The screen could only display a handful of characters; and it had a battery life of only 30 hours. No watch-wearer wants to have to change batteries every couple of days. It soon faced competition from Fossil's Wrist PDA (Personal Digital Assistant), which used the Palm operating system and, with a much larger screen, offered a far greater range of functions. Unlike the Ruputer, however, Fossil's watch lost all data when its battery died. Smartwatches were, after all, still in their infancy; and smarter, smaller watches would eventually bring the genre to maturity.

Today there is great fondness for the original, the HP-01. Collectors can still find one relatively cheaply at an online auction, and there are companies specializing in its repair. One even offers a home repair kit for the nimble-fingered electronic engineer.

'The HP-01 was a scientific wonder capable of complex calculations of time, speed, distance and cost far beyond the basic mathematical functions of its 1975 arrivals.'

Swatch Watch (1983)

Reeling from the collapse of their market thanks to the arrival of cheap quartz watches from Asia, Swiss watchmakers were forced into a new consortium simply to survive. From these desperate times emerged the one watch to save them all.

By the early 1980s, the Swiss horological industry was facing ruin as the public turned its back on traditional watchmaking in favour of the novelty and modernity of quartz. Its bankers were starting to feel nervous and ordered an amalgamation of the two major consortiums of producers. One, the Allgemeine Schweizerischen Uhrenindustrie AG (ASUAG) encompassed Rotary, Rado, Longines, Hamilton, Eterna and other brands. Omega, Tissot and Lemania were the principal members of the other, the Société Suisse pour l'Industrie Horlogère (SSIH).

Both organizations had become insolvent, forcing the banks to take over control of them. At the banks' firm insistence ASUAG and SSIH merged in 1983 to become the Société de Microélectronique et d'Horlogerie (SMH) and the new organization's first CEO, Ernst Thomke, set about restructuring its component parts in the hope of returning them to profitability.

Desperate times require desperate measures, and Thomke's first move was to take on the quartz enemy at its own game. In March 1983, SMH launched a mass-produced quartz wristwatch of its own – the Swatch. The concept had been in development for two years before that date, at Thomke's previous company ETA, who made movements for Eterna Watches, and now he seized the moment.

The Swatch was the antithesis of the luxury sports watches in gold and titanium that some Swiss companies saw as their best hope. Its materials were cheap, mostly plastic; the plastic case was a single piece and there were a total of 51 components in the whole watch, rather than the hundreds that could be found in an upmarket watch of many complications. It was quick to assemble, reducing labour costs to a minimum, and it could, therefore, be sold at a low price, one of the great advantages that the early quartz watches had over traditional Swiss movements.

An affordable product was one thing; but whatever the price tag, the public had to want to buy it. Without the attraction of fine materials and elegant finishes, the Swatch was marketed for its sense of fun, and for its very disposability. Its case might not be gold or silver; its strap might not be leather or steel; its face might do no more than tell the time; but all its parts could be colourful. Plastic, that most versatile of materials, could be dyed; it could be opaque; it could be translucent; above all, it could be printed on.

Above, a selection of relatively sober Swatch watches from its launch in 1983; below, the Swatch Neon Flash Arrow (left) and Neon Wave (right), released in 2024.

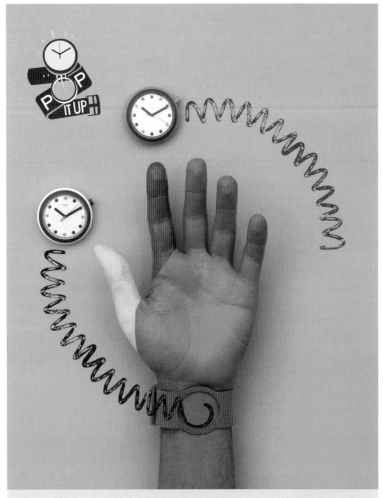

An advertisement for a Pop Swatch collaboration with Malaga-based designer Jesuso Ortiz, in 2017.

CREATE THE UNEXPECTED. #POPITUP
JESUSO ORTIZ × SWATCH

On the production line at Swatch's factory in Sion, Switzerland, a fully assembled Swatch shows all 51 of its components.

The strap and dial were blank canvases for innovative artwork, the like of which had never been applied to a watch before. The strap, previously only a means of attaching the watch to the wrist, was now an integral part of the watch's appearance. Its distinctive attachment to the case, with its extra bridges, was a way of strengthening the connection between two relatively weak materials; but it had the secondary benefit of blurring the distinction between case and strap, allowing designs to flow more easily between the two.

Graphic design was a central element of pop culture in the early 1980s, on everything from T-shirts to album covers. Swatch embraced the fashion, and the youthful market that came with it. The public could buy a Swatch in their favourite colour, or their favourite design; and when they tired of it, they could buy another, or add another to their collection.

The name Swatch was devised by a New York marketing company. It's often assumed that it stands for S(wiss) Watch, but it was conceived from the start as a fashion accessory, to be changed along with one's clothes. One might have a traditional watch for work, or for formal occasions; but the Swatch was to be worn for fun. It was an owner's s(econd) watch, their Swatch. And with a launch price of between CHF 40 and 50, it could be their third and fourth: one early advertisement depicted a wrist wearing three Swatches.

This simple watch, with its versatile appearance, was immediately popular. Another marketing device aimed squarely at a younger generation was the Swatch Club, membership of which offered early access to new designs and limited editions. New Swatch collections arrived with regularity, and they are eminently collectable, discontinued collections even more so. Swatch maintained a core range of around 24 designs, which would remain in its catalogue for two years or so. In addition, however, it released another 24 seasonal designs every three months. On top of these, there were special limited editions commissioned from noted designers, or to coincide with special sporting events. Swatches could easily be produced for organizations and their supporters, and for big occasions such as the Olympic Games.

The first artist Swatch approached to design for them was the French designer Christian Chapiron, also known as Kiki Picasso. In 1984 he produced one design, but in 140 different colourways – enough to drive a serious collector mad. One collector has managed to buy 33 of the variations, each of which, in today's market, can sell for upwards of $25,000.

Buoyed by the success of the Kiki collection, Swatch approached the pop artist Andy Warhol in 1986. He was an obvious choice for Swatch's playful design ethic, but Warhol passed up the opportunity. Instead, he recommended his protégé Keith Haring, a committed populist in the matter of fine art, who leaped at the chance and designed a series of four watches that have become the Holy Grail for many Swatch collectors with their variations on Haring's bold cartoon imagery. Sadly, Haring died, aged 31, in February 1990.

Such was Swatch's success in positioning itself as a fashion accessory that in the 1990s it was introducing new designs almost every week. Having hoped to sell 2.5 million in its first year, it sold its 100 millionth in 1992, only nine years after its launch. Variations on the familiar Swatch began to appear in the 1990s with the introduction of new sizes and additional functions. Swatch Irony, Pop, Chrono, Skin, Maxi, Automatic and Solar collections had all arrived by the end of the last century; the Chrono Plastic, the Automatic Chronograph, the Diaphane collection, the Fun Scuba and the Paparazzi are among many that have debuted since 2000.

One extraordinary collaboration was with the Austrian artist Alfred Hofkunst, who delivered three designs in the form of foods – a dial like a slice of cucumber with a strap like the cucumber's skin; a red pepper whose strap seemed freshly sliced from the side of the vegetable; and a strap of streaky bacon supporting a dial like a fried egg, sunny side up. In each case the strap was irregularly shaped, as you would expect the real thing to be. The collection, titled One More Time, was issued in a limited edition of 9,999 of each foodstuff, and buying a set of all three today will make you wonder why Swatch is regarded as a cheap quartz wristwatch.

Casio F-91W (1989)

It's the best-selling watch of all time and one of the cheapest. Its design has remained unchanged since it was launched over 30 years ago. It is perennially popular with the young, the thrifty and – unfortunately – the terrorist.

Casio was a pioneer in the 1980s of inexpensive, reliable home electronics including keyboard musical instruments, pocket calculators, digital phones and cameras and watches. The F-91W was not its first, but it convincingly established Casio as a player in the market. It was a successor to the F-87W which debuted in 1982 and remained in production for about five years.

At first glance, there is not much to differentiate the two, and internally they boasted the same array of functions – time, date, alarm, chronograph. Visually the most striking feature of the F-91W is the friendly mid-blue line within the bezel that makes the display seem larger than it is. The bezel itself is subtly different from that of the 87W, which was a fairly regular octagon with elongated top and bottom sides. In the 91W, it is more like a square with its corners chopped off; and this small change is the feature of which the watch's designer is most proud.

Ryūsuke Moriai joined Casio in 1985, and the 91W was his first design. The blue line emphasizes the squareness of the layout and gives the whole watch a greater presence on the wrist. The case, like the strap, is made of resin, a material that eventually decays but is cheap to produce. The 91W was designed with a strict set of criteria, balancing function with price point aimed at a very specific sector of the watch market.

The LCD itself is the same size as the 87W's – a six-digit main display showing hours, minutes and seconds, or (in chronograph mode) minutes, seconds and hundredths of a second. The chronograph was upgraded slightly in the 91W, adding net time and split time functions; and the watch could sound an hourly beep, on the hour, to help its wearer keep track of time. A thin outline around the day and date on the 87W was deemed unnecessary for the 91W. A more digitally literate public would not, by 1989, be confused by the two sets of information being so close together.

The controls are the same on both watches, two buttons on the left and one on the right; but the 91W's are set on mounds rather than directly into the side of the bezel. Ryūsuke's greatest challenge in designing the 91W, he has said, was to reconcile the tiny circular battery with the slightly larger octagonal quartz module. The 593 calibre was used for the 91W, replacing the 595 that drove the 87W.

Individually, each of these small changes meant little, certainly to the consumer with no technical or

The 1989 Casio F-91W digital watch, the best-selling timepiece in history, unchanged in over three decades.

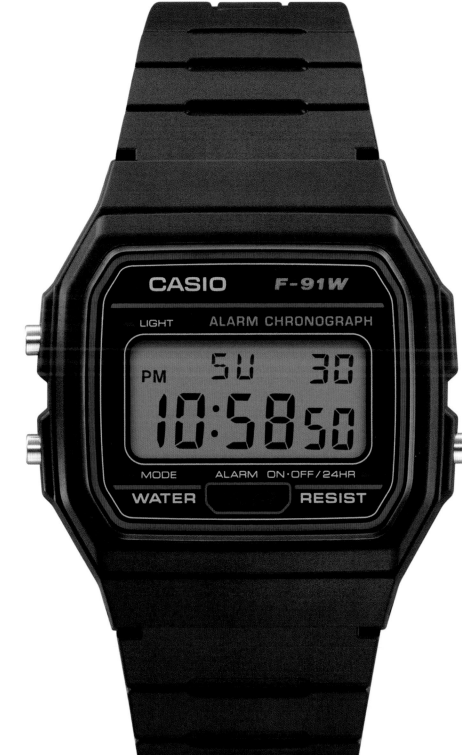

Future president of the United States of America, a young Barack Obama in 1990, wearing a Casio.

Actor Ryan Reynolds emphasizes the ordinariness of his character in the film *Free Guy* (2021) by wearing a Casio F-91W watch.

electronic expertise. As an object lesson in the whole being greater than the sum of its parts, however, the F-91W is perfect. All these incremental improvements simply made for a better watch – better in appearance, better in function, better in value. Modern, digital, plastic, cheap: it was an immediate success with the young in particular, and even now, many years after its arrival, Casio sells about three million of them every year. At a very conservative estimate that amounts to around 100 million over its lifetime so far. It is still in production, completely unchanged from Ryūsuke Moriai's original concept; and in many countries around the world sells for considerably less than it did in 1989. It can cost less to buy a new F-91W than it does to replace the resin strap when it breaks, or the Type 2016 battery when it finally fails – it is expected to last for seven years and there are many examples of the watch running for a decade or more on the same cell.

Ryūsuke still works for Casio. He joined the company just after the launch in 1983 of that other cornerstone of Casio's watch portfolio, the G-Shock. Kikuo Ibe gets the credit for that; but Ryūsuke has been responsible for most of the G-Shock's development and today is its chief designer.

You never forget your first watch, and for many people that was the 91W. No doubt many of its annual three million sales are replacements or sentimental repurchases. It is held in great affection and its ubiquity has imbued it with another characteristic – it is the everyman watch. Those who buy it do so not necessarily because it is the only watch they can afford, but because it is good at what it does, without being big, bold or conspicuously expensive. A young Barack Obama wore one; and the character played by Ryan Reynolds in the gaming world movie *Free Guy*

has a 91W to signify his very ordinariness as a walk-on in a digital role-playing world.

In the real digital world, where watches are connected on the worldwide web, the F-91W is reassuringly unconnected. And there is one sector of society which appreciates that lack of traceability. Members of Al-Qaida and other terrorist organizations want a watch that can't be tracked as they move between secret training camps, covert meeting houses and bomb targets; and one of the 91W's core functions has proved of additional use.

Its 24-hour display means you can set the alarm a full day in advance and, with a little basic electrical knowledge, the watch makes an excellent timer fuse for an improvised explosive device. American Intelligence noticed the presence of fragments of 91Ws at the sites of many bomb attacks and saw so many of the watches on the wrists of suspected terrorists in propaganda photographs (including that of Osama bin Laden) that, in conjunction with other circumstances, the possession of an F-91W can be grounds for reasonable suspicion of links to terror. In more than one instance, a man was arrested when he was found to have two or three of them in his pocket.

As we approach the mid-twenty-first century there may be questions about the sheer disposability of the 91W, whether in an explosion or simply in a waste bin. To compound matters, in addition to the three million produced every year, the F-91W is a victim of counterfeiters, who add to the stockpile with even cheaper imitations. To counter this, Casio has introduced the only change to the specifications of the F-91W in over three decades. If you hold the right-hand button of a genuine Casio F-91W for 20 seconds, the LCD display changes to a friendly confirmation: 'CASIO.'

'You never forget your first watch, and for many people that was the 91W. No doubt many of its annual three million sales are replacements or sentimental repurchases.'

Oakley Time Bomb (1998)

The recession of the 1980s gave way to the affluence of the 1990s, a decade of conspicuous wealth. The rise of the portfolio fashion brand saw many companies expand beyond their original product range into other markets. Could they compete in new sectors without the tradition and experience of long-established leaders?

The traditional watch industry survived the Quartz Crisis by repositioning itself as a symbol of luxury and heritage. The price of really good, well-crafted timepieces soared; and manufacturers of other accessories to life's daily routine looked on in envy. The result was a rush to enter the wristwatch arena with expensive-looking pieces promoted by their association with successful companies in entirely different fields.

The most extreme form of this diversification can be seen in the case of Caterpillar and JCB, both of whom started out as makers of heavy-duty earth-moving vehicles before moving into the arguably related field of rugged footwear and then into watches. Zippo, veteran manufacturer of no-frills petrol-fuelled cigarette lighters, began to make watches – presumably so that, if you smoked, you could have a Zippo in both hands. For Range Rover, the luxury line of the rugged Land Rover vehicle company, watches were a more obvious area for expansion: 'You can afford the car, now buy the watch.'

Oakley also started out in the motor industry, as a manufacturer of hand grips for motorcycles. The company was named after its founder Jim Jannard's dog, Oakley Anne – which was in turn named after Annie Oakley, a rare female star in the world of American Wild West shows in the nineteenth and early twentieth centuries. Annie was a sharpshooter, and her often quoted remark might have served as Jannard's guiding principle: not the one where she declared 'I ain't afraid to love a man: I ain't afraid to shoot him either,' but this: 'Aim for the high mark and you will hit it. No, not the first time, not the second time and maybe not the third. But keep on aiming and keep on shooting for only practice will make you perfect. Finally, you'll hit the bull's-eye of success.'

Jannard guided Oakley from handlebar grips to motorcycling goggles, and from there to skiing goggles, which introduced the brand to a whole new lifestyle demographic. For them he developed the line for which Oakley is most famous, designer sunglasses, the kind you wear on top of your head rather than in front of your eyes. Oakley's trademark look was the horizontal oval lens, and by 1996, the

Back to the future with the Oakley Time Bomb in carbon fibre, a masterpiece of style over content.

Annie Oakley (1860–1926), sharpshooting star of Buffalo Bill's *Wild West* revue, whose name inspired the Oakley brand.

The riveted steel appearance of the Time Bomb's presentation case exaggerated the explosive nature of its contents.

Oakley name was responsible for 15 per cent of the world market in sunnies. Bull's-eye, indeed.

For those who aspired to be wearing their Oakley shades on the lounge terraces of the world's skiing resorts, an Oakley watch (Jannard reasoned) was the obvious and perfect accessory. Oakley launched its first watch in 1998 and called it the Time Bomb. It was, in the same sense that designer sunglasses are so called, a designer watch, designed as graphic art to have a visual impact for art's sake. The Time Bomb, like a real bomb, was designed to be disruptive. It looked unlike any other watch ever made; and with a launch price of $1,500 it was intended to compete against established watch brands Rolex and Breitling in the marketplace.

It certainly caught the eye. The stretched oval case, with its domed glass crystal, followed the curve of the wrist and had the streamlined appearance of a maquette for a Car of the Future. The bracelet looked like the armoured tail of some alien beast designed by sci-fi artist H.R. Giger. Some have compared the Time Bomb to a horseshoe crab crawling over one's arm. It was certainly an alien in the watch world.

It was launched with great fanfare on the wrist of basketball player Michael Jordan, already a brand ambassador for Oakley sunglasses. A pre-launch mail campaign sent out in boxes with the words 'Time Bomb inside', only three years after the dreadful Oklahoma Bombing, had to be hastily abandoned after concerns were expressed by the US Postal Service.

Jim Jannard's eye for impact and his flair for marketing gave the Time Bomb a good start. He loved to tease the public with invented science: Oakley handlebar grips were made, he claimed, of a new compound called Unobtainium; the reflective coating on his sunglasses was, according to the advertising, Iridium – actually one of the 10 rarest elements on Earth; he named another coating Plutonite, although it was actually just a proprietary polycarbonate resin; and the material of which some of his frames were made was the mysterious X-Metal. When it came to the Time Bomb, Jannard claimed that it was driven by a magical Inertial Generator, which sounds like a variation on the Flux Capacitor that powered the futuristic DeLorean time machine in the *Back to the Future* movie franchise.

What Jannard called the Inertial Generator, Seiko – which built and supplied it – called its movement number 5M42. It was the same automatic movement used in thousands of watches badged and branded as in-house products for everything from football clubs to department stores, and sold for a fraction of the Time Bomb's price. It didn't matter. Looks were everything, and the Time Bomb certainly had the looks.

It was followed by similarly stylish watches – the Oakley Torpedo, the Oakley Bullet and the Oakley Jury. They all looked amazing and sat very well alongside Oakley sunglasses and other expressions of the corporate identity. But the watches did not achieve mainstream popularity, and tensions within Oakley led it to issue alongside them more conventional, commercial designs – derivations of the Cartier Tank, for example, or the Rolex Submariner. Oakley was bought out by another eyewear company, Luxottica, in 2007; and although Oakley watch sales were ticking over nicely, the new owners decided to drop the line completely in 2015 and focus on its core business.

At its heart, the Time Bomb was more of a marketing and design exercise than a genuinely innovative watch and, like all such exercises, it came and went. But rarely has such innovative marketing and design been applied to a watch. Oakley watches did look genuinely different from anything else in the market; and their legacy is currently undergoing a reassessment by an Instagram generation with a nostalgic interest in the retro-futuristic fashions of the 1990s from which they emerged.

Ulysse Nardin Freak (2001)

The question of how to display time is an interesting one. The most obvious way, given the mechanical movement of cogs and wheels that drove all watches before the digital age, is a circular dial with rotating hands. The Freak turns all that on its head.

Ulysse Nardin has a chequered and – for a Swiss brand – unusual history, although it began conventionally enough. Its founder Ulysse Nardin grew up in Neuchâtel, an area of northwest Switzerland from where so many great watchmakers originated. Like others he learned his craft in the long winters when farming was impossible, and farmers took on piecework for the local manufacturers. Ulysse studied under his father Léonard-Frédéric Nardin, and set up his own eponymous company in 1846, at the age of 23.

Land-locked Switzerland has produced many great horologists; but Nardin may have been the first to demonstrate a fascination with the sea. He specialized in pocket marine chronometers, essential equipment on which navigators relied to plot their longitudinal positions. Despite growing up in alpine meadows rather than by ocean shores, Nardin was so confident about his timepieces that he took them to the Great Exhibition in London in 1862, a display of the best of British and international manufacturing at

the height of the Industrial Age. In a field dominated by Abraham-Louis Breguet and his English counterpart John Arnold, Nardin won the top prize for Complicated Watches and Pocket Chronometers.

By the twentieth century, Ulysse's son Paul-David Nardin had succeeded him and guided the company to further successes at the Paris Exposition Universelle of 1889, the Chicago World's Fair four years later, and others. Thanks to the success in Chicago, he began to supply the US Navy from 1902, and the navies of Britain, Russia and Japan soon joined his list of clients. In all, more than 50 naval forces around the world have adopted Nardin chronometers.

The company suffered like all others during the Quartz Crisis and in 1983 it was put up for sale; Swiss businessman Rolf Schnyder jumped at the chance. Schnyder had been working in the Swiss watch industry since the late 1950s when he joined Jaeger-LeCoultre's advertising department. He moved to a distribution company delivering watches to Asia and was so enamoured of the region that he settled there, opening factories in Thailand and Malaysia that supplied watch parts to Swiss producers.

Although he had never worked directly with watch design or manufacture, Schnyder understood the business well and saw a market for something that Ulysse Nardin had never produced – wristwatch-sized

2001's Ulysse Nardin's Freak –
a watch with no crown and a
dial with no hands.

The back of the Freak, revealing the huge spring that gives the watch seven days' running.

Ulysse Nardin's Trilogy of Time – left to right: the Tellurium Johannes Kepler, the Planetarium Copernicus and the Astrolabium Galileo Galilei.

versions of its pocket marine chronometers. Schnyder worked with master watchmaker Ludwig Oechslin; and the revived company debuted with a spectacular trilogy of watches with astronomical complications, now known as the 'Trilogy of Time'.

The Astrolabium Galileo Galilei, named after the Italian astronomer, was the first of the trilogy, released in 1985. Displaying not only terrestrial time but that of the heavens, the Astrolabium also tracked the phases and eclipses of the Sun and the Moon and the movements of several of the greater stars on which sailors traditionally relied for navigation. Incorporating 21 separate functions, it was named the world's most functional watch by the *Guinness Book of Records* in 1989.

The Astrolabium was followed in 1988 by the Planetarium Copernicus, and in 1992 by the Tellurium Johannes Kepler, both with similarly complex complications. The Tellurium (from the Latin *tellus* meaning Earth) had a cloisonné dial; each one took 50 hours of a craftsman's time to make, putting it through 12 heat processes and 54 individual stages of manufacture. Every single Tellurium is unique.

The Freak arrived in 2001, truly a freak: a watch with no crown and a dial with no hands. It was designed to make a splash, but it was no gimmick. Ludwig Oechslin, who had masterminded the complexities of the Trilogy, had designed a watch in which the movement, completely visible beneath the dome of the crystal, rotates not hands but itself. Parts of it point to the bezel, from which the time can be read. To adjust the time, one simply rotates the bezel.

To wind the watch, one turns the back of the case in the direction of a small arrow. An aperture in the back offers a glimpse of the large spring, covering almost the entire diameter of the watch, which gives it seven days of power.

Switzerland's Fondation de la Haute Horlogerie, a society for those at the highest levels of watchmaking, declared the Freak its Watch of the Year in the Innovation class. Not only did it turn the whole relationship between movement and display on its head; the movement itself was a pioneering first. Traditional watches use jewels because they are hard-wearing and smooth, reducing friction and prolonging the life of a movement. Oechslin was, with the Freak, the first designer to use silicon instead. Not only is silicon as smooth and robust as jewels, but it can also be moulded to any shape. These qualities allowed Oechslin to completely reinvent the escapement, the ticking regulator that lets the movement move at a fixed rate. Using silicon he was able to make a twin-wheel escapement instead of the usual single wheel, attached with four points instead of two, with greater stability and no friction. Nowadays, everyone is doing it, but Nardin did it first.

Oechslin went on to found his own company, Ochs & Junior, in 2006, specializing in watches with astronomical complications. After Schnyder's death in 2011, his wife sold the company to the French luxury goods brand Kering. Kering divested itself of Ulysse Nardin and its other watch brand Girard-Perregaux via a management buy-out, restoring Ulysse Nardin to independence once more.

'Switzerland's Fondation de la Haute Horlogerie, a society for those at the highest levels of watchmaking, declared the Freak its Watch of the Year in the Innovation class.'

Hublot Big Bang (2005)

Following a trend set by Audemars Piguet and Patek Philippe, Hublot's first watch was inspired by *un hublot* – a porthole, in French. Industry insiders were unimpressed, but the public liked it; and since then the company has become a byword for watches that you either love or hate.

At a time when many Swiss watch companies were still going out of business in the wake of the Quartz Crisis, it was a brave man who started a new one. That man, in 1980, was Carlo Crocco, an Italian watchmaker who left Breil in 1976 to start his own company in Nyon, on the shores of Lake Geneva.

Crocco's first design, the original Hublot, was launched at Baselworld 1980, to supreme indifference; he didn't sell a single watch on the first day of trading. The porthole, the bezel of the watch, had 12 visible screws around its perfect circle – arguably an old trick first seen years earlier on the Audemars Piguet Royal Oak. A shallow protrusion on the left side, mirrored by the crown guard on the right, was a reference to the hinge and fastener seen on actual ships' portholes – a feature first incorporated into Patek Philippe's Nautilus.

The Classic, as it was known, was a bold fusion of high-status gold, in its case and bezel, with a very ordinary material, natural rubber, for its strap. Today we are accustomed to all manner of straps in leather, PVC, silicone, real leather, precious and un-precious metals and combinations of many of them. In 1980, however, it was little short of scandalous to demean a gold watch with such a commonplace strap, at least within the rarified atmosphere of Baselworld.

Outside, however, it was 1980. The punk movement in popular music was already on the wane, being replaced by New Wave and the New Romantics. Punk music may have been yesterday's news; but its iconoclastic approach lived on, admired and adopted by a new, younger generation of watch buyers. Beyond Baselworld, sales of the Classic picked up and brought Crocco sales in the first year of $2 million.

Crocco remained at the helm of Hublot until 2004 but found that administrative duties were increasingly distracting him from the pleasure of watchmaking. He handed the reins over to Jean-Claude Biver, then president of Omega, a man with a reputation for shaking things up and refreshing tired or defunct brands. Biver picked up on the Classic's fusion of old gold and new rubber, and defined Hublot's style as 'art in fusion'.

This principle was put into action with Hublot's next range of watches, launched late in 2004 – the

The Hublot Big Bang, with Hublot's trademark porthole face and rubber strap, whose line continues around the side of the case.

As a Hublot ambassador, athlete Usain Bolt arrives for the opening of Hublot's flagship Fifth Avenue store in New York on 19 April 2016, wearing not one but two of the company's watches.

The Hublot Classic Fusion from 1980, the company's first wristwatch, which scandalized horological society with its combination of expensive gold and cheap rubber.

Big Bang. Biver retained the trademark porthole, now with six visible screws; and a layer of Kevlar along the side of the case, in the same colour as the strap, gave the impression that the strap ran right through the body, a rare moment of joined-up thinking in an otherwise disconnected appearance. He threw together a diverse set of colours and elements – stainless steel, gold, tungsten, carbon, magnesium, Kevlar, ceramic and even rubber – in a wilfully iconoclastic approach to watch design.

The Big Bang is a watch designed to provoke. It won the prize for Best Design at the Grand Prix d'Horlogerie de Genève 2005; and Hublot's core demographic of post-punk 25- to 45-year-olds took to it very quickly. By the end of the Big Bang's first year, the company's sales had quadrupled. Watch purists took a different view – there was no art in this fusion of random natural and manmade stuff, no concept except anti-concept. The Big Bang, they insisted, was gauche, ugly – and even if it was fun, that didn't mean it was good. Fast food is fun. Battle lines were drawn and have remained in place ever since.

The Big Bang has been through innumerable changes since it first appeared, and sometimes the only constant seems to be its ability to mutate. It has appeared in dials of 38mm, 41mm, 44mm (the standard diameter) and, as the Big Bang King diver's watch, 48mm. The round bezel has been included with and without its visible screws, and sometimes (as in the Spirit of Big Bang) been dropped altogether in favour of a tonneau outline. It has been purple, lilac, pale blue, royal blue, at least two shades of green, red, white and all-black. A steady stream of limited editions seems designed solely to part collectors from their money.

Hublot collectors are a specific breed. While other brands are amassed as investments, Hublot fans like the Big Bang for its sense of irreverent fun, and, mischievously, for the very fact that some people can't stand it. As one (50-year-old) Hublot collector remarked when asked why he chose Hublot over, say, Patek Philippe: 'Hey, I'm not 80!'

The brand knows its young market well. Hublot chooses to sponsor public figures renowned for their sporting prowess and maverick characters: the fastest man in the world Usain Bolt; the world's greatest tennis player Novak Djokovic; legendary footballers Pelé and Diego Maradona, and football managers José Mourinho, Gareth Southgate and Didier Deschamps.

Since Hublot introduced a women's version of the Big Bang in 2008, women now account for 28 per cent of the company's sales. Hublot has also recruited tennis players Simona Halep and Elina Svitolina, and outstanding footballer Ada Hegerberg, as ambassadors. One unfortunate Friend of the Brand was Bernie Ecclestone, then chief executive of Formula One motor racing. Ecclestone was mugged by a gang of men who stole his Hublot Big Bang. With Ecclestone's permission, Hublot used the incident to its advantage and ran an advertisement showing Ecclestone's face covered in bruises. The slogan accompanying the picture said: 'See what people will do for a Hublot.'

'The Big Bang is a watch designed to provoke. It won the prize for Best Design at the Grand Prix d'Horlogerie de Genève 2005; and Hublot's core demographic of post-punk 25- to 45-year-olds took to it very quickly … Watch purists took a different view.'

Bulgari Octo Finissimo (2014)

'You can never be too rich or too thin.' Truman Capote claims he was the first to observe this, although the aphorism has been attributed to everyone from Dorothy Parker to the Duchess of Windsor. The phrase is usually applied to wealthy socialites, but it might easily be describing the Octo Finissimo.

The Octo Finissimo's roots go back, like those of so many iconic watches, to Gérald Genta, the visionary behind the Audemars Piguet Royal Oak and the Patek Philippe Nautilus. Genta designed watches for his own, eponymous company as well as for others; and the eight-sided form that inspired the Royal Oak and the Nautilus resurfaced in 1991 with the Gérald Genta Octagonal. Compared to the earlier models, the Octagonal series was flamboyant and richly complex, as befits the style of a designer moving on from the 1970s to the 1990s.

Genta sold his company in 1999. After a brief ownership by a distribution company, it wound up a year later in the hands of Bulgari, the fashion brand that is a byword for Italian dash and panache. The firm's roots are actually Greek, as it was founded by Sotirios Voulgaris, who grew up in Kallarytes, an ancient centre of silversmithing in mainland Greece.

Voulgaris moved to Rome, Italianized his name and opened a jewellery shop there in 1884. The Bulgari business prospered, and to emphasize its 'Italianness', it adopted the Latin form of the letter U, a V, for the shopfront of its new flagship store in Rome in 1934. The spelling has become the Bulgari logo and is often used, as Bvlgari, in lifestyle magazine articles out of respect for the brand.

As the new owners of Gérald Genta, Bulgari now had the rights to many of Genta's inspired movements, complications and case designs, including the octagonal geometry on which Genta had so often riffed. The first fruit of the new ownership was the Gérald Genta Octo range. Although it might be considered an obvious step to piggy-back on Genta's trademark octagon, the Octo was a genuine development of it, a true progression.

Its defining feature was a stepped, architectural bezel, which some have likened to a Mayan temple: first, an octagonal case, a square with cut-off corners; on top of that is a shorter, more regular octagon, set in slightly from the edge of the case at the top and bottom, and defining the shape of the watch face; and, finally, fitting perfectly between the inner and outer edges of the higher octagon, a perfect circle, serving to emphasize the straight-sided forms below it. The circle gives the Octo a sense of conformity,

Gérald Genta's design for Bulgari, the Octo Finissimo – an octagon within a circle within an octagon, on display at Baselworld 2019.

Actor Bradley Cooper flashes his Octo Finissimo at a Bulgari promotional event in Paris in 2013.

The skeletal Octo Finissimo Tourbillon automatic wristwatch houses Bulgari's thinnest movement yet, only 1.95mm in depth.

which only a closer inspection of the edges of the octagons dispels. Thus the watch manages to appear conventional while being quietly disruptive underneath.

Bulgari trumpeted this as the modifying influence of Italian style on Swiss innovation. Italy gives us refined fashion – exquisite suits, for example – but rarely anything to redefine the genre. An Italian suit is still recognizable as a suit; an Italian supercar is still a conventional car, albeit a magnificent one. The Octo was a very high-spec watch, and unmistakably a Genta, but it was not technically radical.

That would change. A succession of superficial redesigns of the Octo followed over the following 10 years, as is usual with successful and even unsuccessful models – having spent the costs of development, any watch house seeks to recoup them. But fashions change over 10 years, and in the second decade of the twenty-first century there was a move away from the chunky sports watches that had dominated the market for 40 years, toward a slimmer model. Bulgari determined that the next Octo would follow this trend – and not just follow it, but lead it.

Finissimo means either 'most fine' or 'most thin' in Italian. The two have often been synonymous in the world of jewellery and other accessories where delicate work was the mark of a master craftsman. The Octo Finissimo was well named in either sense. From the front it had the same impactful appearance as its predecessors in the series, but sideways on it measured a mere 5.15mm in depth.

It was a masterpiece of reduction, made possible because Bulgari owns all the facilities that produce the various stages of manufacture, and can insist on what the design demands. The Finissimo is genuinely made in-house – even if all the Italian house's watch workshops are actually in Switzerland. Within the case, the movement itself is only 2.23mm deep, and the dial a paper-thin 0.2mm. For comparison, the average USB cable is 3mm in diameter.

The Octo Finissimo has become a range in its own right, with several variations. Some of them, such as the Octo Finissimo Repeater, with the addition of gongs to the movement, clock in at a bulky 6.9mm deep. The Octo Finissimo Tourbillon Automatic, launched in 2018, overcompensates for the Repeater's lapse, beating Bulgari's own record for thinness at a skinny 3.95mm, of which the movement accounts for just 1.95mm – less than the thickness of two CDs.

Who wears a Finissimo? It seems to be attractive to a certain type of thinking action hero, as played by Gerard Butler, Bradley Cooper, Jeremy Renner, Jared Leto and others. Finesse, it seems, attracts finesse.

Whether or not you like the appearance of the Octo line, the technical innovation required to manufacture and assemble its Finissimo models in all their shallow intricacy is impressive. The Finissimo variations have won more than 60 awards for what goes on beneath the dial. The current top of the range is the Bulgari Octo Finissimo Perpetual Calendar Haute Horlogerie, a platinum body on a blue alligator-skin strap with a blue dial and the additional complication of a full calendar function, stretching the watch's depth to 5.8mm. This watch will set you back rather more than $100,000. It may be true that you can never be too rich or too thin, but if you want to be very thin, you must expect to come away a little less rich.

'Its defining feature was a stepped, architectural bezel, which some have likened to a Mayan temple ...'

Apple Watch (2015)

It's hard to overstate the impact of the Apple Watch, not only on the watch industry but on the world. Just as the first wristwatch changed our relationship with time and the first mobile phone changed our relationship with the rest of the world, so the Apple Watch changed our relationships with our watches and phones, thus changing everything.

The Apple Watch brought together so many different functions that it threatens to make almost all our other devices obsolete. However, in many cases it wasn't the first to do some of the things it does. Arguably the first smartwatch was Hewlett-Packard's HP-01 in 1977 (see page 110). Casio and Pulsar introduced watches that could receive and store personal information in the 1980s. The FitBit revolution in wrist-worn fitness and health trackers began in the 1990s. Apple's own iPod played our favourite music whenever and wherever we wanted. But the Apple Watch was a portal to all this, and everything else.

Apple didn't really know what it wanted a watch to do when it set out to develop one in late 2011. It was the first Apple project to be conceived entirely without the input of Steve Jobs, Apple's inspirational founder who had died in October 2011. But the company had looked into the future and decided that the next step was for technology to move on to the body. By 2011, people were beginning to realize just how much they were allowing their mobile phones to run their lives, and to resent the fact. If the iPhone was a rather detached, impersonal interface with daily life, perhaps a watch – more intimately connected to our bodies – might present a more human, more personal connection.

Apple's first concept was for a sort of glass iPod bangle wrapped around the wrist, and, in its early stages, it was going to use the same interface and apps as an iPhone; but as part of the humanization of the device the developers focused on a more streamlined interaction. The result was the Apple Watch, a sophisticated gatherer of information about the wearer's usage and health, which it can analyze and display. It also makes calls and tells the time.

As well as the now familiar interaction of tapping on a touchscreen, a second layer of connection called Force Touch enables the user, by pressing the screen more firmly, to access further functions of the watch. Sensors on the base of the watch collect information about the physical condition of the wearer, another human touch. The watch also contains a barometer, gyroscope and accelerometer, to help it understand the environment around it and

An original Apple Watch Sport from 2015, when it changed forever our relationship with physical activity.

Always ahead of the curve, *Vogue* US editor-in-chief Anna Wintour attends a fashion event in Los Angeles on 16 April 2015 wearing an Apple Watch, three days before its launch.

Two examples of the Apple Watch series 10, unveiled in September 2024. The watch has so many apps now that it can be just about anything its owner wants it to be.

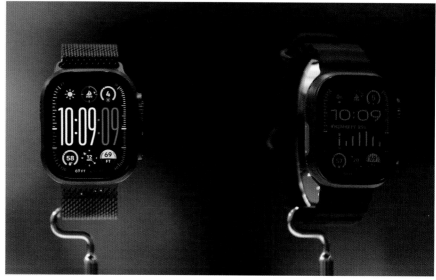

get its compass bearings. Data from the various sensors is relayed to the user's iPhone for analysis and the results are sent back to the watch to display to the wearer. In the absence of an iPhone, the watch can also connect directly with the internet.

The health and wellbeing functions of the Apple Watch were not a primary consideration when it was first conceived. Apple was more concerned about improving the wearer's relationship with their iPhone. The health-monitoring capacities are, however, a very great benefit to users. The Apple Watch can take electrocardiogram (ECG) readings and later models of the watch can also monitor blood-oxygen levels. It is a formidable, powerful device, and obviously much, much more than a timekeeper.

Apple has a legion of devoted admirers and a long history of making accessibility a key component across all its products. The launch of the Apple Watch was therefore guaranteed to attract enormous attention. To avoid unmanageable crowds queuing outside Apple Stores around the world, it was, at first, sold only online – enthusiasts were able to see demonstrations of its abilities in-store, but had to order via their iPhones or iPads. The first Apple Store to carry the watch as stock was the Colette store in Paris.

In the first full financial quarter after its launch on 19 April 2015, 4.2 million Apple Watches were sold. By the end of the year it was double that, and the rate increased steadily through to 2022, when annual sales peaked at 53.9 million. Although annual numbers have fallen slightly since then, it's now estimated that more than 80 per cent of iPhone owners also have an Apple Watch. By the end of 2024, Apple expects to have sold in total around 303 million watches.

Not everyone owns an iPhone, and not everyone wants an Apple Watch. Even so, the Apple Watch accounts for a remarkable 30 per cent of the smartwatch market. Falling sales year on year since 2023 may reflect a growing sense among the public that, for all the interest that the Apple Watch takes in our health, wellbeing and other aspects of our lives, it can be an unhealthy obsession. Apple Watch-wearers, it's been estimated, consult their watches 80 times a day; and an increasing number of people, especially among the young, are turning away from smartwatches and smartphones in general, in favour of 'dumb phones' that don't do much except make phone calls, and certainly preserve a greater level of the user's privacy.

If there's a backlash against a dependence on high-tech gadgetry to relieve us of our life skills, perhaps the same trend will see a return to simple watches. Although a fine mechanical timepiece is by no means low-tech, it is often a thing of great beauty and fine human craftsmanship, both inside and out. And unlike quartz watches, Apple Watches and smartphones of all kinds, it will never run out of power. Perhaps there's something to be said for tradition after all.

'If the iPhone was a rather detached, impersonal interface with daily life, perhaps a watch – more intimately connected to our bodies – might present a more human, more personal connection.'

Index

Picture Credits

About the Author

Colin Salter is a science and history author and bibliophile living in Edinburgh, Scotland. He has written the *Science is Beautiful* trilogy (Batsford Books), *The Anatomists' Library* (Ivy Press) and is the lead author of Pavilion Books' '100s' series, which includes *100 Books, 100 Symbols* and *100 Science Discoveries that Changed the World*. His book *The Moon Landings* (Flame Tree Publishing) celebrated the fiftieth anniversary of the first man on the Moon. He has contributed to guidebooks on seashells, leaves and birdwatching, and with Michael Heatley he was co-author of *Everything You Wanted to Know about Inventions*. He has also written extensively about travel and popular music.
www.colinsalter.co.uk